BORN TO BE FREE

BORN
TO BE FREE

Discovering Christ's Power
to Set You Free
from a Painful Past

TOM VERMILLION

NEW YORK

BORN TO BE FREE
Discovering Christ's Power to Set You Free from a Painful Past

Disclaimer: The Publisher and the Author make no representations or warranties with respect to the accuracy or completeness of the contents of this work and specifically disclaim all warranties, including without limitation warranties of fitness for a particular purpose. No warranty may be created or extended by sales or promotional materials. The advice and strategies contained herein may not be suitable for every situation. This work is sold with the understanding that the Publisher is not engaged in rendering legal, accounting, or other professional services. If professional assistance is required, the services of a competent professional person should be sought. Neither the Publisher nor the Author shall be liable for damages arising herefrom. The fact that an organization or website is referred to in this work as a citation and/or a potential source of further information does not mean that the Author or the Publisher endorses the information the organization or website may provide or recommendations it may make. Further, readers should be aware that internet websites listed in this work may have changed or disappeared between when this work was written and when it is read.

Unless otherwise noted, Scripture quotations are taken from the Holy Bible, New International Version, © 1973, 1978, 1984 by The International Bible Society. Used by permission of Zondervan Bible Publishers. Scripture quotation marked KJV is taken from the Holy Bible: King James Version. Scripture quotation marked NKJV is taken from the Holy Bible, New King James Version, © 1979, 1980, 1982 by Thomas Nelson, Inc., Publishers. All stories related in this book are based on actual events but names have been changed to maintain confidentiality for those involved.

ISBN 978-1-61448-604-6 paperback
ISBN 978-1-61448-605-3 eBook
ISBN 978-1-61448-606-0 eBook
Library of Congress Control Number: 2013933176

Morgan James Publishing
The Entrepreneurial Publisher
5 Penn Plaza, 23rd Floor,
New York City, New York 10001
(212) 655-5470 office • (516) 908-4496 fax
www.MorganJamesPublishing.com

Cover Design by:
Chris Treccani
www.3dogdesign.net

Interior Design by:
Bonnie Bushman
bonnie@caboodlegraphics.com

In an effort to support local communities, raise awareness and funds, Morgan James Publishing donates a percentage of all book sales for the life of each book to Habitat for Humanity Peninsula and Greater Williamsburg.

Get involved today, visit
www.MorganJamesBuilds.com.

Habitat for Humanity®
Peninsula and
Greater Williamsburg

CONTENTS

ACKNOWLEDGEMENTS

I want first of all to thank Jesus for the incredible patience and grace that He has extended to me time and again throughout my life. Also my wife Susan, a genuine blessing from God, for her constant encouragement and support. Thanks also to my amazing daughters Amity and Tiffany who have stood by me and encouraged me as well through the years.

In addition I want to express thanks to Pastor Kevin York who invited me to be part of his church staff in 2004, which opened the door for the development of the ministry out of which this book was birthed. Thanks as well to Pastor Daniel Stephens for his encouragement and support and to numerous friends in the Lord who, for years, have been a constant in my life and who have, from time to time, pulled me out of the ditch when I wasn't paying attention.

Also to our Freedom Ministries team as we have learned together how to point others to God's amazing love and freedom.

PREFACE

Every believer's birthright in the Kingdom of God is freedom and healing—both physical and emotional. Scripture emphatically declares that Jesus came to heal the brokenhearted and to set captives free from every form of bondage. If that is true then ...

- Why are so many Christians still in bondage to anger, bitterness, addictions, depression, and relational brokenness?
- Why do destructive behaviors devastate Christian families from generation to generation?
- Why do so many Christian marriages end in divorce even after dozens of sessions with Christian counselors and therapists?
- Why do so many Christians experience minimal life transformation after coming to Christ?

Born to be Free will give you insights and spiritual solutions for these questions and more. It will provide a balanced biblical theology for healing, freedom, and transformation in the kingdom of God. Having done that, it will then walk you through a proven process for experiencing healing from brokenness, freedom from your past, freedom for your present, and the transformed life seen on the pages of the New Testament.

If you are a follower of Jesus Christ, you possess a birthright of healing and freedom that far too many Christians have yet to experience. Jesus did not die on the cross so that we could merely manage crippling and destructive issues in our lives, but so that each of us could be set free from bondage and brokenness. The promise is this: "So if the Son sets you free, then you will be free indeed" (John 8:36). As you read this book you are invited to partner with God in experiencing the life Jesus has purchased for you on the cross.

This is not the first or only book on these matters. There are great books that fully develop each of the biblical truths I will share with you but this book will give you a foundational overview of the Holy Spirit's tool box for setting God's people free. This book contains the biblical principles that are the heart of our Freedom Ministries at Mid-Cities Community Church. We have seen hundreds of lives transformed by the blood of Christ and the power and authority he has delegated to those who follow him and who want more. This is not for highly anointed believers but for ordinary followers who will take Jesus at his word. Christ has already done the work; we simply call forth what he has done.

At the end of each chapter you will find a few questions for journaling and reflection. It is a form of meditation which in Hebrew thought carries the idea of "chewing on something" for a while. I hope you will take advantage of these opportunities to explore the biblical concepts presented in the chapter and to hear from the Holy Spirit as he leads you into all truth just as Jesus promised. There will also be a memory verse that will help write God's truth on your heart and sometimes a suggested prayer.

In a sense, this is a book and a manual. Part 1, *The Promise of Freedom*, is the theology and methodology for finding healing and freedom in the Kingdom of God. Part II, *The Process of Freedom* is essentially a manual of prayers and declarations to guide you through the process of healing and breaking the power of the enemy. For some reason, God has directed me to write this book. Perhaps you are that reason.

May the Lord give you the Spirit of wisdom and revelation as you seek to know him more through this book.

THE PROMISE OF FREEDOM

Chapter One

AMBUSHED

Now to him who is able to do immeasurably more than all we ask or imagine... (Eph. 3:20)

I have served as an associate pastor in conservative, Bible believing churches for over thirty years. Much of my ministry was given to counseling individuals and married couples from my congregation and community. I consistently struggled with two issues in that part of my ministry: the level of brokenness in the Body of Christ-even for longtime believers—and the powerlessness I felt on too many occasions to truly help. In counseling sessions, I could accurately identify the issues and give people insights about their struggles, but I had no tools or techniques to profoundly touch the deeply wounded places from which all their destructive behaviors continued to spring. Many of the people I worked with were sincere believers who had been in and out of counselor's offices for years but had never truly gained victory over their "issues." Even the Word and prayer could not seem to overcome the brokenness in these individuals which eventually seeped like toxic waste into their relationships — especially marriages.

Disconnect

Deep inside, I sensed a huge disconnect between what I saw on the pages of the New Testament and life in my church. What I saw on the pages of Scripture were radically changed lives. I saw the Apostle Paul, miraculously transformed himself, writing to once profoundly broken people at Corinth who then seemed to have been truly set free to grow in Christ. There was no mention of professional counselors or an expectation that people could learn to "manage their issues" over a period of months or years. There was no sense that addictions could only be dealt with through residential programs in mental health facilities followed up by years of support group involvement. There was no hint that homosexuals were hopelessly locked into a life determined by genetics or that a myriad of psychological and emotional issues could only be managed with drug therapies. What I saw in Scripture was the Body of Christ and the Holy Spirit doing life together and people being truly set free and transformed.

> Do not be deceived: Neither the sexually immoral nor idolaters nor adulterers nor male prostitutes nor homosexual offenders nor thieves nor the greedy nor drunkards nor slanderers nor swindlers will inherit the Kingdom of God. **And that is what some of you were** (emphasis added). But you were washed, you were sanctified, you were justified in the name of the Lord Jesus Christ and by the Spirit of our God. (1 Cor. 6:9-10)

Here Paul lists the same issues that torment us today—sexual immorality, gender confusion, substance abuse, materialism, criminality, etc. But he declares that through Christ, lives had been changed and identities transformed. Brokenness was relegated to the past and now these believers truly walked in newness of life. They were, indeed, new creations. Ragtag fishermen now stood before governors as ambassadors for the Kingdom of Heaven, sleazy tax collectors became radical philanthropists overnight, and the "Mary Magdalene's," once demon possessed, were now fully possessed by God.

For me, there was a great gulf between what I read and what I saw. In my heart, there was always a longing for more. But I had been trained not to expect "more" and that if I did see "more," I was to be suspicious. My church's theology presented a gospel in which God, in an orderly universe, had ceased dispensing miracles and radical life change long ago. The pages of the New

Testament were full of promises and stories that truly did happen — but only in the days of Jesus and the apostles. I intuitively sensed, however, that if you jettison the miracles, you also jettison the power and in doing so you quench the Holy Spirit and neuter his ministry. I, however, needed power in my own life as much as the wounded people I served.

An older man in our city named Bill ran a yellow clapboard mission where materials about the power of the Spirit were given away and prayers for healing and deliverance from demons were practiced in back rooms. John, a friend of mine and a leader in my church, was also longing for a gospel with power. John became friends with Bill and began to frequent the clapboard mission. One day John invited me to have lunch with him and Bill. At that time, my view of "charismatics" was not favorable — emotional people with bad theology, bad hair, and plaid coats asking for money or tossing snakes around. But, because of my friendship with John I reluctantly agreed.

Bill was not what I expected. He was thoughtful, articulate, knew Scripture, and seemed "normal" in every sense. He gave biblical answers to my questions about the supernatural and about the demonic. I was given a few tapes, which I took back to my office in a plain brown wrapper. I listened to them with my door closed. I wasn't a convert, but I was beginning to see some solid biblical foundations for the continuing supernatural ministry of the Holy Spirit.

One windy spring day, a very polite, professionally dressed young woman walked into our offices to see a minister. She was directed to me and cautiously sat down in an old brown leather chair across from mine. Her name was Elizabeth and her first words were to the point: "What do you know about demons?" My response was not to the point. "Why do you ask?" She seemed unaware that a Christian pastor might think that talk about demons was bizarre, so she calmly continued to lift the curtain on her life.

Two years earlier, she had joined a "witch's coven." At first, she said, it was exhilarating and intriguing. But the coven had recently taken a turn to the darker side of the dark side. Animal sacrifices and discussions of human sacrifice were more than she had bargained for. When she attempted to leave the coven, she was informed that coven membership was for life…at least until "death do us part." She felt that the coven leaders were not serious but only trying to draw her back through intimidation. There was, however, something that did frighten her. Elizabeth became visibly tense as she told me about repeated appearances of demons in her bedroom at night. These manifestations filled her with feelings of fear and dread that she couldn't shake.

I began to wonder just how stable Elizabeth was, but her calm demeanor and rational tone made it hard to dismiss her. Then she asked, "What can you do about these demons?" What struck me was her expectation that any church leader should be able to deal with these issues, as if it were part of our normal ministry routines. Obviously, she wasn't acquainted with our church. Our entire answer to the demonic was that we didn't believe in it, therefore, we didn't need to do anything about it. Suddenly, I had an inspired thought! I would take her to Bill in the old mission downtown and let him work with her. She agreed. I drove my car and she drove hers.

On the way, I determined to introduce her, release her into Bill's capable hands (dump her), and leave knowing that I had fulfilled my pastoral duty. We arrived. She told Bill her story. He and his ministry partner agreed to take her through deliverance, if she was willing. Bill was matter-of-fact. Elizabeth was agreeable. I was looking for an open exit door. My strategy to cut and run suddenly hit a snag. As I began to excuse myself, Bill simply told me that I wasn't leaving. Since I brought Elizabeth, I needed to stay and minister deliverance with them. I earnestly explained that I had no competence in this particular field. Bill said, "Fine. You can sit there and pray while we deliver." Trapped, I dutifully sat down. Immediately, I began to wonder if demons were indeed real. More importantly, if they were real, where might these dislodged demons land? I uncomfortably imagined myself as prime real estate for their relocation.

My next great hope was that nothing at all would happen. I would not be infested and I could go back to my office knowing that all this was well-intended emotionalism run amuck. Bill began with a prayer for protection. So did I...with my eyes open. As Bill began to invoke the name and the blood of Jesus, to bind the enemy, and to command demons to come out of this young woman, I saw several things that had not been part of my experience until that moment. Elizabeth morphed from a quiet, petite lady to a brazen woman with an arching back and a rebellious, mocking laugh. Her body stiffened. Her dark eyes took on an amber hue. Over the next hour, I witnessed shrieking, nausea, gagging, and more laughter. But one by one, these manifestations ceased and at the end of an hour I a saw a woman exhausted, but at peace. Fear was gone and she had named Jesus as her Lord rather than the dark prince of this world. She drove away and I never saw her again. My world had changed. I had been ambushed by God.

Over the next few months, God sent several people to me that I did not ask for. I made numerous trips to Bill's mission. I was not excited, and yet, I knew that God was beginning to move me into "the more" that I had wanted and prayed for. In those months, I saw people set free in short order from fear, pornography, lesbianism, rage and other issues that I could not have accomplished with my counseling techniques in months or years. And even then, I could only have brought them to a place of managing the issue rather than being free. The pages of Acts began to come alive to me and the authority and victory of Jesus became an experiential reality.

Since then, God has led me into a very different approach to ministry and counseling. It has born tremendous fruit. Jesus always shows up and always amazes me. This is not a blanket rejection of counseling techniques used by therapists in the church or community. Many of those techniques are built on solid research and do help. But they can only touch a person in the natural realm. Rarely do they address the spiritual realm and the things that impact us that are rooted in that realm. That leaves a huge gap, since Paul himself declares, "our struggle is not against flesh and blood, but against...the spiritual forces of evil in the heavenly realms" (Eph. 6:12).

Personal Reflection / Journaling:

- When have you wanted or needed a powerful move of God in your life? Did your faith and understanding of God's ways help or hinder God moving on your behalf?
- What areas of your life are not yet submitted to Christ? What has kept you from overcoming that issue?
- If you could ask God to heal any part of you or your life what would it be?

Suggested Prayer:

Father in heaven, I want more of you, more of Jesus, and more of your Spirit. Show me what I need to know to receive everything Christ has purchased for me with his blood. Give me greater faith, greater understanding, and a greater portion of your Spirit. Holy Spirit, watch over me as I read this book and highlight those things that are most important for me to understand and receive. Jesus, guard my heart and mind so that I receive nothing that is not from you. I pray these things in Jesus' name...Amen.

Memory Verse:

"I pray also that the eyes of your heart may be enlightened in order that you may know the hope to which he has called you, the riches of his glorious inheritance in the saints, and his incomparably great power for us who believe." (Eph. 1:18-19)

Chapter Two

BORN TO BE FREE

Where the Spirit of the Lord is, there is freedom. (2 Cor. 3:17)

The gospel is about freedom in Christ. According to Scripture, it is the right of every believer. The new birth is intended to be a birth into freedom. There are dozens of scriptures in the New Testament that use the language of freedom in reference to our relationship with Christ. It is a biblical expectation that people will be set free from all the things that limit their ability to be pleasing to God and to experience the abundant life that Jesus promises. In this chapter, I want to confirm for you that God's will for his people is not just the forgiveness of sins but also radical transformation in the lives of his children. Sometimes, freedom comes through an event, while at other times it comes through a process. But the promise is for every child of God. It is our inheritance.

Another Gospel

"I am astonished that you are so quickly deserting the one who called you by the grace of Christ and are turning to a different gospel — which is really no gospel at all." (Gal. 1:6-7)

In the early stanzas of Paul's letter to the Galatians, he scolds the church for being so easily seduced by a "different gospel." False teachers had come in shortly after Paul left the city and had begun to preach that the Law of Moses was still essential to salvation. They were not denying the messianic role of Jesus but were declaring that, in addition to faith in Jesus, circumcision and scrupulous keeping of certain other parts of the Torah were also necessary for salvation. Paul warned them that a gospel based on anything other than faith in the risen Son of God was no gospel at all. A gospel that is just another form of law keeping is not good news at all since it puts the burden of salvation back on man's performance rather than on what the Son of God has done for us.

"Another gospel" was created in Galatia by adding elements that God had not ordained. It is also possible to create "another gospel" by omitting or minimizing elements of the gospel of Jesus Christ. In many churches "another gospel" has been unintentionally preached for decades. These churches have faithfully declared the forgiveness of sin in the name of Jesus, but too often have not emphasized in meaningful ways the transforming power of Jesus Christ in the lives of believers. A gospel that does not declare and demonstrate power to destroy the works of Satan in a person's life is not the gospel preached by Jesus, nor the early Church.

After John the Baptist was imprisoned by Herod, he sent his disciples to Jesus asking him if he was, in fact the Messiah, as John had originally thought, or if there was to be another. Apparently John himself had a preconception of the Kingdom of God that did not match what he was seeing or experiencing personally. Jesus answered by saying: "Go back and report to John what you hear and see: The blind receive sight, the lame walk, those who have leprosy are cured, the deaf hear, the dead are raised, and the good news is preached to the poor. Blessed is the man who does not fall away on account of me" (Matt. 11:4-6).

Jesus defined his ministry and the gospel he preached by the power it unleashed on the earth to radically change lives. Paul declared, "For the kingdom of God is not a matter of talk but of power" (1 Cor. 4:20). Any gospel falls short if it speaks only of the forgiveness of sin in this world while relegating the hope of healing and transformation only to those who have already crossed the threshold of heaven. The gospel Jesus preached is the coming of the Kingdom of God on this earth and our entry into that kingdom now by the blood of Christ. In that kingdom, transformation is the rule, not the exception.

If we are honest, many believers today are saved but remain in bondage to sin, addiction, shame, and a host of other hindrances to their walk. The truth is that other than church attendance, a large percentage of believers look just like the people they work with or go to school with who do not have the Spirit of Christ living in them. Divorce rates in the church rival divorce rates in the culture at large. Christian teens seem to have little power over the cultural pressure to drink, experiment with drugs, or to be sexually active. A significant number of believers live on antidepressants, tolerate marriages dominated by anger and rage, live with bitterness toward the past, and are crippled by an overpowering sense of unworthiness and rejection. I'm not scolding these brothers and sisters for not being "the Christians they should be" because I have struggled with many of those issues as well. These believers are desperately looking for freedom, but in many cases have not been shown by their churches how to access the freedom that Jesus promises.

A gospel that only gets us to a place of forgiveness but that does not radically change us so that we stand out in contrast to our culture is not the gospel of the kingdom that Jesus preached. Paul pointed to this truth when he said, "Do everything without complaining or arguing, so that you may become blameless and pure, children of God without fault in a crooked and depraved generation, in which you shine like stars in the universe as you hold out the word of life" (Phil. 2:14-16). Stars stand out in stark contrast to the darkness. Jesus himself declared that his followers were to be the light of the world. Those who wear the name of Christ should stand out in the crowd by their sheer "differentness." Jesus spoke of being "born again" not as figurative language for trying harder but as a reality where something real and essential has been altered in everyone who comes to him. After a while, that essential difference should become apparent, not a as a reflection of our efforts but as a reflection of the power of God working in us and Christ being formed in us.

Luke tells us that shortly after forty days of fasting and temptation in the wilderness, Jesus returned to Galilee in the power of the Spirit. On the Sabbath he returned to the familiar synagogue in which he was schooled as a boy growing up in Nazareth. It was customary for guests, which included former members of the synagogue, to be given the honor of reading publicly from the Torah. Whether Jesus requested the scroll of Isaiah or whether God orchestrated the moment, we don't know. However, Jesus purposefully unrolled the scroll to the section that we designate as Chapter 61. Jesus read aloud the words of Isaiah that would describe the messianic mission of the Son of God. When he finished the reading, he sat down and said, "Today this scripture is fulfilled in your hearing" (Luke 4:21).

Luke seems to give an abbreviated reading of Isaiah, but let's look at the full text that Jesus would have undoubtedly read to those in the synagogue that day.

> The Spirit of the Sovereign LORD is on me, because the LORD has anointed me to preach good news to the poor. He has sent me to bind up the brokenhearted, to proclaim freedom for the captives and release from darkness for the prisoners, to proclaim the year of the LORD's favor and the day of vengeance of our God, to comfort all who mourn, and provide for those who grieve in Zion — to bestow on them a crown of beauty instead of ashes, the oil of gladness instead of mourning, and a garment of praise instead of a spirit of despair. They will be called oaks of righteousness, a planting of the LORD for the display of his splendor. (Isa. 61:1-3)

As Jesus read this text, he was issuing the mission statement for his kingdom enterprise and for the Church that would continue to fulfill the mission after his ascension. In this statement, he outlines the focus of his ministry on planet earth. When John the Baptist asked if he was the Messiah, Jesus answered him by saying that he was doing the very things that Isaiah had foretold about the Messiah. John sums it up simply in his first letter when he says that Jesus came to destroy the works of the devil" (1 John 3:8).

Marching Orders

Jesus began by declaring that the Father had anointed him for a purpose. Wherever there is an anointing there has already been an appointing. When God sends any of his people on a mission, he gives them the power and authority to carry out the mission. When Jesus sent out the twelve and then the seventy-two to preach the good news, he gave them power and authority to preach, heal, and deliver as they went. The Father had done the same for Jesus as he embarked on his mission. So in the synagogue in Nazareth where Jesus spent much of his early life, Jesus unveiled the *marching orders* he had received from his Father.

He began by naming a group that has always been near to the heart of God — the poor. It was to the poor that Jesus would typically preach his good news. The poor, primarily, are the ones eager for change since the rich are usually content with the status quo. The ministry of Christ extends God's kingdom blessings to the poor, the weak, the broken, the sorrowful, the oppressed, and the down-and-out of this world so they may have standing in the Kingdom of God. The amazing news that God was finally beginning the invasion he had promised, to liberate the planet from an oppressive enemy, was initially declared to a young virgin of little means in Nazareth. Next it was spoken to a working class stiff, a carpenter by trade, who was engaged to the young girl. Later, on the very night of the birth of the anointed one, angels declared the good news to scruffy shepherds sleeping on the ground who also perched on the lower rungs of the Israeli socioeconomic ladder.

In many ways, the gospel was preached primarily to the poor because they were more open to the message. Jesus came proclaiming a kingdom that would not resonate with those who already had heavy investments in the systems of this world. Jesus came declaring a kingdom whose real estate would be the hearts of men rather than prime property just off the interstate, a kingdom that began first with surrender rather than conquest, and a kingdom built on love for enemies rather than hatred and revenge directed toward oppressors. The ministry of Jesus would be unveiled, not to the wealthy or the powerful, not to the celebrities or the politicians, but to the ordinary and even to the less than ordinary that walked the earth. For those of us who have ever wondered if God could value us since the world does not, Jesus answers with a resounding, "Yes."

The next part of his mission statement goes deeper. He has been sent to bind up the brokenhearted. The psalmist writes, "he heals the brokenhearted and binds up their wounds" (Ps. 147:3). Ezekiel uses the same language in God's rebuke to the shepherds of Israel who had not cared for the weak or impoverished. In that text, God says, "I will search for the lost and bring back the strays. I will bind up the injured and strengthen the weak" (Ezek. 34:16). A central part of the mission of Christ, then, is not just to preach but also to heal both our physical brokenness and the emotional, psychological, and spiritual wounds deep within each of us. A gospel that has no power to heal these pockets of pain is not the gospel Jesus was anointed to preach.

In the next verse, Jesus declares that he has come on a rescue mission to liberate those who are behind the wire in the "reeducation camps" of the enemy — to declare freedom for the captives and release from darkness for the prisoners. Jesus has come for those who have no power to escape, no bribe to open a door, and no friends in high places to pull strings. Jesus, through the prophet Isaiah, spoke of both prisoners and captives. The idea of prisoners is that these individuals have gone through a legal process, have been found guilty and then have been sentenced. Captives, on the other hand, have been overpowered and enslaved by an enemy.

To restrain sin, God established a law of reciprocity for all men: "Do not be deceived...a man reaps what he sows. The one who sows to please his sinful nature, from that nature will reap destruction; the one who sows to please the Spirit, from the Spirit will reap eternal life." (Gal. 6:7-8) Many of us, if not most of us, have become prisoners through our own decisions. God has clearly told us there are consequences to our choices — we will reap what we have sown. If we live by the flesh we will make decisions that, in the short run, seem to be in our best interest. In the long run, however, these decisions end up taking us to places we never wanted to go. Sometimes we become prisoners of those outcomes.

Jesus spoke of such consequences in Matthew 18. This entire chapter is dedicated to relationships and primarily how we should respond to others in light of what God has done for us. Beginning in verse 21, Jesus tells the story of a servant who had borrowed a huge amount of money from his master. When the master ordered an audit, the servant was called before him and ordered to repay the debt. The servant who had incurred the debt had absolutely no ability to repay. So the master, according to his legal rights, ordered that all of his possessions be liquidated and his wife and children sold into servitude until the debt could be repaid. The desperate servant begged for mercy. In an amazing gesture of kindness and generosity, the master completely forgave the debt.

Nearly every first time reader of this story would expect this man to leave the presence of his master full of thanksgiving and joy, with a lifelong commitment to generosity toward others. But instead, he rushed out to find a fellow servant who owed him a few dollars and demanded immediate payment. When his fellow servant couldn't pay, the one who had been forgiven an unpayable debt had the other man thrown in jail. When the master heard what had happened, prompted by righteous anger, he turned the unforgiving servant over to tormentors to be tortured until his first debt was fully paid.

The unforgiving servant became a prisoner by his own refusal to respond to the kindness of his master and was subject to the tormentors as a consequence. When we choose to live independent of Jesus or even hold back parts of our lives from Jesus, we may find ourselves living in darkness, isolated from those who would love us, tormented by our own self-hatred, and eventually living a life full of regrets. We may even be subject to the torment of demonic spirits who have attached themselves to us as we have walked in sin and rebellion.

Of course, there are also the more obvious prisons brought on by choices that have led to crippling addictions, guilt, and tormenting shame over sinful behaviors never brought to the cross. Many believers who have come to Christ are still prisoners of their past. They are unaware of the power Jesus offers to set them free and send them on their way. Only the cross and the blood of Christ can reverse those trends in our lives and set us free from prisons we have fashioned by our own choices.

Then there are the captives who, in many cases, have been victimized. These are the ones who have been attacked by the enemy and subjected to bondage. They have no power to free themselves, but Jesus has come to set them free. Many were taken captive as children through abuse, abandonment and neglect. For years they have been held captive to lies that were sown deep within them. The lies fill them with shame, condemnation, fear, unworthiness, and a host of other toxins that constantly seep from their wounds. Their captivity to these wounds keeps them from giving love or receiving love as God intended. We will talk about these issues in depth later in this book but for now, it is enough to say that there are still many captives in a kingdom that promises freedom.

Christ's mission is still to set prisoners and captives free from their past and to heal hearts — even those that have been hardened by pain. As you read the remainder of the Messianic text in Isaiah, you see that the resounding chorus is the word "instead." God is willing to replace one thing with another. Christ has come to reverse the fortunes of all who hear the gospel. Those full of sadness will find reasons to rejoice. The beaten down will become more than conquerors. Lives that lie in ruin will be rebuilt, and where the darkness of depression once reigned, God's light will shine. These promises are not for those who walk the streets of gold in heaven, but for those who are slogging knee deep through the muck of this world.

Jesus did not declare a kingdom that was coming "one of these days" but a kingdom that had indeed come back to planet earth as the Father had foretold through his prophets. This was the core of the good news of the Kingdom of God that John preached and Jesus fulfilled. It is a gospel of transforming power that is for now as well as for the eternal age to come. It is a gospel filled not only with grace to take away sins but also with power over the enemy, power to heal, power to restore and power to set free.

Again, a gospel without power to set people free, not just from the legal consequences of sin in the heavenly courts, but from the bondage of sin and brokenness in their lives falls short. A body without muscle and blood is only a skeleton like the dry bones of Ezekiel's vision (Ezek. 37). Structure without power only lies in the dust. When the power of the Spirit of God came upon those bones they were raised to life and became an army. Jesus said over and over again that the marks of the Messiah, his Church, and his kingdom were the manifestations of power for healing, radically changed lives, and for setting people free from bondage and darkness.

To take away these manifestations of God's kingdom on earth by relegating them to centuries past leaves us with a church without the power of God to change a person at his core. It leaves people with a church that leads them instead to make mere external changes that fail in times of crisis. The local church can do many things with excellence and even with passion. We can offer amazing messages, creativity, world class music and drama, effective inner city ministry, goodwill, great marriage conferences, excellence in psychological counseling, moral teaching and smoking recovery groups. All of these things have the capacity to produce good and can demonstrate God's love. But all of those things can be done within the strength, creativity, passion and intellect of men. God, however, wants to do a work over which he can declare, "'Not by might nor by power, but by my Spirit,' says the Lord" (Zech. 4:6).

Only Jesus can restore sight to the blind, hearing to the deaf, truly break the power of addiction, cast out demons, and change hearts as well as behaviors. Paul, an accomplished student of Rabbi Gamaliel, discovered that sobering truth in Athens. There, in the face of intellectualism and religion, the apostle pulled out his most compelling outlines, launched his best arguments and articulated a reasoned gospel with eloquence. At the end of Acts 17, Luke tells us that after all of Paul's efforts, only a few men became followers. Apparently, Paul had trusted in his education, his powerful intellect and his creative messages. But he left disappointed. His next stop was Corinth. Paul had settled on a very different strategy for that city: "When I came to you, brothers, I did not come with eloquence or superior wisdom as I proclaimed to you the testimony about God. For I resolved to know nothing while I was with you except Jesus Christ and him crucified…My message and my preaching were not with wise and persuasive words, but with a demonstration of the Spirit's power" (1 Cor. 2:1-2, 4). The gospel of power and transformation that Paul preached turned Corinth upside down.

Whatever we do for God in our own strength, Satan can probably do better. Whatever we do for God that is out of our own capacity will probably not measure up to those empowered by the prince of this world. Hollywood, Nashville, and Las Vegas can produce breathtaking shows that distribute their message around the world in a few days. Barnes & Noble is filled with books by capable writers who capture the imagination of men and profoundly shape their world-view. The sections devoted to those books far outnumber the Christian book section. Secular universities, think tanks, and researchers wow the crowd everyday with new discoveries and medicines that promise healing. Without the supernatural power of God, we can't measure up.

The kingdom, however, is not about the best that man can do. The kingdom is about the best that God can do. It is about the power of God pushing back the borders of Satan's territory. It is about the power of the Holy Spirit being expressed through his Church and the Kingdom of God being advanced on this earth by that power. Jesus framed the movement of the kingdom this way, "From the days of John the Baptist until now, the kingdom of heaven has been forcefully advancing, and forceful men lay hold of it" (Matt. 11:12). The substance of the Kingdom of God is the power of God being expressed in ways that set us free from everything that hinders our relationships with God and with one another. Men who desperately want God grab hold of it.

On several occasions, Jesus was asked to identify the greatest commandment. He always answered that the greatest commandment was to, "Love the Lord your God with all your heart and with all your soul and with all your mind and with all your strength" (Mark 12:30-31). He would then volunteer that the second greatest commandment was similar to the first, "Love your neighbor as yourself."

In John 13, Jesus raised the bar considerably. There he now commanded us to love one another just as he loves us (John 13:34). Neither of these commands can be obeyed without the power of God working in us in transformative ways. Neither can be done without the heart, soul, and mind being profoundly healed by the power of God. Forgiveness gives us the desire to love God but the transformative power of the Spirit gives us the ability to love God…and others.

We ask broken people to love one another, forgive adultery, and release years of verbal abuse in their own strength. And they want to, but they can't. Jesus has to enter in and supernaturally heal broken hearts, deposit love for God and love for others, and take the blinders off in the spiritual realm so that we can see ourselves as God sees us — and Jesus will. That is the gospel of Isaiah that Jesus declared in Luke 4. It is Jesus standing at the door of our hearts knocking—waiting to be invited in so that he may transform the interior of each of his followers by healing broken hearts, setting captives free, opening eyes to the truth of God's love and breaking the power of the enemy. It is his transforming gospel of freedom.

Freedom

There are numerous scriptures in the New Testament that speak about freedom in Christ. I have listed a few of these passages to simply confirm in your spirit that God is serious about setting you free. I have already mentioned some of these but want to reinforce God's heart about your liberation before moving on.

> The Spirit of the Lord is on me, because he has anointed me to preach good news to the poor. He has sent me to proclaim freedom for the prisoners and recovery of sight for the blind, to release the oppressed, to proclaim the year of the Lord's favor. (Luke 4:18-19)

> When Jesus saw her, he called her forward and said to her, "Woman, you are set free from your infirmity." Then he put his hands on her, and immediately she straightened up and praised God. (Luke 13:12-13)

> To the Jews who had believed him, Jesus said, "If you hold to my teaching, you are really my disciples. Then you will know the truth, and the truth will set you free." (John 8:31-32)

> Jesus replied, "I tell you the truth, everyone who sins is a slave to sin. Now a slave has no permanent place in the family, but a son belongs to it forever. So if the Son sets you free, you will be free indeed. (John 8:34-36)

Therefore, there is now no condemnation for those who are in Christ Jesus, because through Christ Jesus, the law of the spirit of life set me free from the law of sin and death. (Rom. 8:1-2)

It is for freedom that Christ has set us free. Stand firm, then, and do not let yourselves be burdened again by a yoke of slavery. (Gal. 5:1)

Now the Lord is the Spirit, and where the Spirit of the Lord is, there is freedom. (2 Cor. 3:17)

In summary, these scriptures make it clear that freedom is a major theme in the atoning work and ministry of Jesus. Not just freedom from the penalty of sin but from sin itself in all its manifestations: condemnation, shame, sickness, addiction, spiritual blindness, demonic affliction, deception and so forth.

These passages also tell us that freedom is not the absence of something as much as it is the presence of Jesus. This makes perfect sense. Where Jesus is present, there is peace, wholeness, love and security. Where Jesus stands, heaven is present. Freedom is not the idea of living without restraint or un-submitted to anyone or anything. True freedom is not freedom from restraint but freedom to love and be loved in its fullest sense. We get there not by focusing on the enemy, self, or our brokenness. Rather, Scripture tells us to make our primary focus Jesus. We are to behold him, fix our eyes on him and consider him. As we fill our lives with his presence and purposes, the enemy is displaced and the vacuum filled with the Spirit of Christ.

Lord and Savior

A major hindrance to freedom that I have observed in myself as well as in others is that while we are quick to accept Jesus as Savior, we are much slower to accept him as Lord. But freedom and transformation require both. I cannot even begin the journey of change without the power of sin being broken in my life by the blood of Christ. When I come to Jesus and his Spirit is deposited in me (Acts 2:38), God's power is available to be released in me in ever increasing amounts. However, the release of that power is conditional. As faith is the condition for our initial salvation, faith and obedience are the keys to power and transformation in our lives.

Jesus said, "If anyone loves me, he will obey my teaching. My Father will love him and we will come to him and make our home with him" (Jn. 14:23). "I am the vine; you are the branches. If a man remains in me and I in him, he will bear much fruit; apart from me you can do nothing." (Jn. 15:5)

There are several implications of the words Jesus spoke in these passages. First of all, the evidence of our love for him is our willingness to be obedient — to keep his commands. Many of us declare our love for Jesus but then live a life based on our own agendas. I don't mean that we live an overtly sinful life, but we live a life dominated by worldly or self-interests. We rarely ask Jesus to show us his will. We forge ahead instead, asking him to bless what we have decided to do. We often pursue the "good things" the world offers rather than seeking first the Kingdom of God and his righteousness, and we often compromise with the world to get ahead and get along.

Ultimately, I think it is because we don't fully trust him to always act in our best interests or fully believe that his commands will lead us to the abundant life he promises. Much of what Jesus calls us to do is counterintuitive and paradoxical. To be first you must be last. To be the greatest you must be a servant. To save your life you must give it up. We may give some kind of intellectual assent to these verses but if we are honest, in our hearts we are not so willing to place ourselves fully in the hands of Jesus.

Only through a kind of reckless obedience do we discover that Jesus is absolutely trustworthy and that every promise is true. Jesus must not only be Savior but also Lord if we are to fully experience the freedom and the blessings that are ours in him. Submitting both our external and our internal worlds to him is needed. As we continue to surrender more of ourselves to him, we experience more of him. With him come purpose, joy, healing, freedom, peace, power, and everything else that resides in heaven. Whatever we hold back from his Lordship continues to keep us in bondage and puts us at risk.

A single school teacher named Amanda set up a time to visit with me about "some spiritual questions" she had. Amanda's concern was that she felt God was no longer responding to her prayers. She had been raised in church, was faithful in her attendance, and taught children's Bible classes in her church. God had clearly answered her prayers in the past but lately her prayers felt as if they were just dropping to the floor like pigeons flying into a window.

I asked, "What are you asking God for that he has been silent about?" Amanda told me about her most urgent prayer. She had been in a clandestine relationship with a married man with children for several years. For the last year or so, she had been praying fervently that he would divorce his wife and marry her as he had promised. He had taken no action and she was frustrated that God was not moving on a request that was so important to her. I asked Amanda why she thought God would answer a prayer for a husband to leave his wife and children for another woman. Her theology was simple: "The Bible teaches that God wants me to be happy and that is what would make me happy. So God should answer my prayer."

Amanda had not submitted this part of her life to Christ. To do so opened her up to a strong deception. Not only was she violating the will of God, but she was also asking God to be a co-conspirator in her sin, which would devastate a man's wife and children for years or generations to come. When we are loose with the lordship of Jesus in our lives, viewing him as our servant rather than our Lord, we push out into dangerous waters. Without a constant commitment to trust Jesus and grant him lordship over every part of our lives, we risk giving the enemy a place to deceive us and may find ourselves paying a huge price for the deception. As I discussed Amanda's flawed theology with her, she quickly saw the deception and repented, but she had certainly lost ground in her spiritual life.

My point is that when we fail to surrender areas of our lives to Christ, we hinder the work and revelation of God within us. It is easy to believe that because I have surrendered certain parts of my life to Jesus, that every part of my life is surrendered. Yet, nearly all of us maintain personal sovereignty over bits and pieces of our hearts or lives because we are afraid to entrust them to Jesus. Those places we refuse to surrender then become the very pockets that keep us from finding the freedom and love God wants us to experience.

The saddest thing in the Kingdom of God is the reality of churches and believers who have been full of potential for years but then essentially remained the same, experiencing little of the destiny written for them in God's book. The psalmist said, "All the days ordained for me were written in your book before one of them came to be" (Psalm 139:16). God has already determined everything that he has for us. Yet when we live forgiven but not transformed, much of what is written will simply become footnotes of what might have been.

Freedom Is Only in Christ

The most important truth is that the freedom God promises is only *in Christ* and is only found in the presence of his Spirit. "Where the Spirit of the Lord is, there is freedom" (2 Cor. 3:17). Those who are not in Christ do not have the Spirit of Christ within them and so cannot fully experience this freedom (See Rom. 8:9). I have prayed with many people who have ongoing struggles with issues in their lives that made no real progress in their walk with the Lord. Many have been in church most of their lives and have been puzzled about their inability to "get through to God." It is not that God doesn't hear their prayers but that he has appointed his Spirit to accomplish his transforming work in our lives. Without his Spirit within us, most of that work will remain undone.

Many people who see themselves as followers of Christ have made commitments to a church or have lived out the faith of their parents or spouse but personally, they have never really submitted themselves to the lordship of Jesus. They have not received salvation on the basis of their own personal faith in Christ and his sacrifice rather than on their good works or the works of their church. They have entered into religion with every good intention but not into a relationship with the Lord himself. These individuals may be nice, live relatively moral lives, and volunteer in their community but they have no personal walk with the Lord. Because of that, they do not have the Spirit of Christ within them to pray on their behalf nor to do his transforming work. "In the same way, the Spirit helps us in our weakness. We do not know what we ought to pray for, but the Spirit himself intercedes for us with groans that words cannot express. And he who searches our hearts knows the mind of the Spirit, because the Spirit intercedes for the saints in accordance with God's will" (Rom. 8:26-27).

Many people assume that because they attend church or even read their Bible on occasion, Jesus understands their intentions and counts them as his. Couples can date for years with the intention of marrying some day and can even live in the same house, but no one is married until intentions are declared and vows are spoken. To borrow a slice of theology from *The Princess Bride*, Wesley tells Buttercup when she is about to take her life (because she assumed she had been married to the evil prince), "If you didn't say it, you didn't do it." Coming to Christ requires more than an intention or an understanding, it requires a declaration. In Christ are all blessings and the transforming power of heaven, but they are not ours until we enter into a covenant by our own faith and declarations. When by faith we personally accept the sacrifice of Jesus on our behalf and confess him as Lord and Savior, we receive his Spirit to live within us and the ministry of his Spirit makes all the difference.

If you are not certain about your relationship with Christ, make sure that you have responded to Christ's invitation, as God would have you respond. If you have not done so, you may receive Jesus as your Savior and the Lord of your life now. We receive salvation simply by believing that Jesus Christ is the Son of God and responding by faith to what he has done for us (John 3:16). Jesus came into this world in the flesh as one of us, lived a sinless life, and then suffered and died on a cross to pay the penalty of death that was assigned to our sins (Phil. 2:6-11). The great mystery is that as Jesus represented the human race before the Father, he was charged with our sin while we were credited with his righteousness. We are saved by God's grace through our faith based totally on what Jesus has done for us and not on the basis of anything we have done (Eph. 2:8). Believing this, we are to turn from a life of willful sin, confess Jesus as the Lord of our lives, and surrender our lives to him.

Having done that, his Holy Spirit takes up residence within us to help us live for him and become like him. If you accept these things by faith, yet never personally responded to Jesus and asked him to be your Lord and Savior, I encourage you to do that now by praying the following prayer. (Remember, this is not about what you have done. It is all about what he has done for you.)

Prayer for Salvation

Heavenly Father, I confess that I am a sinner in need of your grace and forgiveness. I believe that Jesus Christ is your Son, that he lived in the flesh and died in my place, taking my sin and my guilt upon himself. I believe he was raised from the dead on the third day and ascended to heaven where he waits to return and claim his own while judging the wicked. I now renounce sin and all the works of Satan. I acknowledge Jesus as my Lord and Savior and promise to live for him each day of my life. I ask for your Holy Spirit to live in me and make me into the image of Jesus Christ. Thank you for making me your child by the blood of your Son, Jesus. In the name of Jesus, I now receive total forgiveness for my sins and rejoice in your grace and mercy. It is in his name that I pray...Amen.

Personal Reflection / Journaling:

- What part of Jesus' mission statement out of Isaiah 61 do you need most in your life?
- For you, what does freedom in Christ mean?
- What areas of your life currently seem bound up or seem to hinder your joy and your ability to give or receive love?

- Which of your recurring behaviors is not submitted to Christ?
- Which areas of your emotions or thought life are not yet submitted to Christ?
- What did God deposit in your heart as you read through this chapter?

Suggested Prayer:

Father in heaven, your desire is for me to be free and to fully know the freedom that your Son has purchased for me through his suffering. In the name of Jesus, I submit my behaviors, my emotions, my thought, and my past to you and ask Jesus to take Lordship over each of those areas. I entrust myself to you and ask that you begin to show me each day the way to freedom. I ask these things in Jesus' name...Amen.

Memory Verse:

"Where the Spirit of the Lord is, there is freedom." (2 Cor. 3:17)

Chapter Three

THE VIOLENT KINGDOM

From the days of John the Baptist until now, the kingdom of heaven has been forcefully advancing, and forceful men lay hold of it. (Matt. 11:12)

During a period of forty days following his resurrection, Jesus appeared to his followers on numerous occasions. What he spoke about had to be critical to the success of those he left to complete his work. What he spoke about had to be the things that burned in his heart more than anything else. Luke tells us that spoke about the Kingdom of God. I am convinced that a biblical understanding of the Kingdom of God is essential for healing, freedom, and the life Jesus wants us to live. This chapter is about that kingdom and its relation to the transforming power of Jesus Christ in our lives.

The Kingdom

The Kingdom of God was the central message of the preaching of John the Baptist, then of Jesus, and then of the Church. The phrase "Kingdom of God" is used sixty-eight times in the New Testament. The synonymous phrase "kingdom of heaven" is used thirty-two times by Matthew. Both John the Baptist and Jesus proclaimed that the Kingdom of God was near. The meaning was that even as they preached, the Kingdom of God was within reach for those who would take hold of it. "From the days of John the Baptist until now, the kingdom of heaven has been forcefully advancing, and forceful men lay hold of it." (Matt. 11:12) The word translated "forcefully" or "forceful" in the NIV is such a strong word that some translations use the term "violent." It carries the idea of unleashed power from heaven and the idea of men and women pursuing that kingdom with everything they have…all their heart, soul, mind, and strength.

Jesus not only proclaimed the kingdom but demonstrated its presence. People's lives were drastically changed by what he preached. Sinners gave their hearts to God. Faith erupted. The blind threw down their canes, the lame listed their cots on eBay, and the formerly demon-oppressed brought whole regions to faith. Jesus declared and demonstrated that a major reconstruction of the earth was underway that would soon post a sign, "Under New Management."

What is the Gospel of the Kingdom?

The gospel that Jesus was sharing was not yet his death, burial and resurrection. Although the message of the kingdom was based on what Jesus would soon do in history and what had already occurred in the mind of God (Rev. 13:8), it was a message that encompassed much more than forgiveness of sins. The key to understanding the Kingdom of God is found in what is commonly referred to as the "Lord's Prayer" (Matt. 6:9-13). In that prayer, Jesus instructs us to plead, "Your kingdom come, your will be done on earth as it is in heaven." Heaven is the place where God reigns and where his will is perfectly manifested in every heart and every action. In heaven, God's children experience love, joy, peace, health, security, strength, significance, abundance and freedom. It is also a place where God's children do not experience shame, rejection, abuse, violence, bitterness, debilitating pain, disease, hunger or want.

Christians often believe that the kingdom of heaven exists only in the spiritual realm, "somewhere out there" to be experienced by believers as they step out of their mortal body. Yet Jesus said that the Kingdom of God was already a reality on earth when he walked among us in the flesh. Praying for the continued expansion of his kingdom on earth is to be a central part of our prayer life. Although the Kingdom of God is not yet experienced on earth in its fullest sense, Jesus said that since his coming, the kingdom has been advancing on this earth person by person, heart by heart, and that the evidence of it is seen in lives that are being redeemed and reconfigured by the power of God.

This gospel affects everything. If the Kingdom of God has come to earth then so have the power and the blessings of that kingdom. Through Christ, both power and blessing have been made available to the children of God and citizens of heaven who currently reside on the earth. They have been made available not only to radically alter the individual lives of believers but also to be used by them to push back the borders of darkness in this world. In the ministry of Jesus and the early church, there was a definite pattern. Preach the good news of the kingdom. Heal the sick. Cast out demons. Raise the dead. That pattern is seen over and over in the ministry of Jesus and in the ministry of the Church.

> Jesus went throughout Galilee, teaching in their synagogues, preaching the good news of the kingdom, and healing every disease and sickness among the people. News about him spread all over Syria, and people brought to him all who were ill with various diseases, those suffering severe pain, the demon-possessed, those having seizures, and the paralyzed, and he healed them. (Matt. 4:23-24)

John summed it up simply, "The reason the Son of God appeared was to destroy the devil's work" (1 Jn. 3:8). Jesus also said: "As the Father has sent me, I am sending you" (John 20:21) and, "I tell you the truth, anyone who has faith in me will do what I have been doing. He will do even greater things than these, because I am going to the Father" (John 14:12).

Simply put, Jesus came to earth to destroy everything the devil had done to the Father's planet by replacing the devil's works with the works of God. Broken lives, bondage, disease and affliction — these things are not the will of God because they are not found in heaven. The culture of the Kingdom of God has no place for these tormentors. Therefore, Jesus and his Church have been given power on earth to heal broken hearts and set captives free. What Jesus began, he expects us to finish, as the power of heaven is made available to us through him. That is the gospel of the kingdom.

Scripture echoes again and again the truth that the blessings and resources of heaven are available to its citizens now.

> But our citizenship is in heaven. (Phil. 3:20)

And my God will meet all your needs according to his glorious riches **in Christ** Jesus. (Phil. 4:19)

I pray also that the eyes of your heart may be enlightened in order that you may know the hope to which he has called you, the riches of his glorious inheritance in the saints, and his incomparably great power for us who believe. (Eph. 1:18-19)

If we believe that God's goodness, power, and extreme blessings are only reserved for those who have died and are now resting in paradise, we will have no expectation for God to move in power on our behalf or on behalf of his church. We will expect only the ordinary and pray only for the ordinary.

How often do we only trust God to work through ordinary or natural means — doctors, therapists, medications, or technology — rather than trusting him to move in supernatural ways? I am not saying that we should not go to doctors or take medications. Those things are a grace of God for a fallen world. But they are a lesser grace, primarily for those who have not yet accessed the blessings of heaven through Jesus. The question is whether we ever actually ask God in faith to move supernaturally before settling for what he provides in the natural. Jesus defined the kingdom by the supernatural moves of God, not just his kindness expressed in the natural.

The feeding of thousands recorded in Mark 6 is a perfect example. After hearing Jesus teach all day, the crowds were hungry. His disciples saw two solutions in the natural realm, to either find enough money to buy food for the people, or send them away to find their own. Jesus had them take an inventory and found that five small loaves of bread and a couple of small fish were all that the crowd offered up. The disciples viewed their problem and their resources in the natural but Jesus examined the situation with kingdom economics. As he blessed the food, his prayer and confidence in his position as a Son of his heavenly Father transferred their limited resources from the kingdom of men to the Kingdom of God. There the Father has unlimited resources for his children. The result was an over abundance of food to meet the need. Too often we still ask God to answer our prayers in the natural rather than through the supernatural provision of heaven come to earth.

Kingdom Mind-set

Sometimes, we push back against the idea of submitting to Christ and allowing him to be formed in us. We are afraid of losing ourselves. Spiritual transformation is not about giving up who we are, but about discovering who we were truly meant to be. Freedom is not the absence of obstacles or restraint in our life, but is the life of Jesus Christ operating in us to bring us into the fullness of our destiny.

To a great extent, this spiritual metamorphosis is about coming to understand who we already are in Christ and living with the perspective of "sonship" rather than "slaveship." Many believers still view themselves as the same people they were before coming to Christ…only forgiven. Many of us are focused on the obstacles in our life. We think about our past hurts, our present pain and the bondage that grips us. The enemy works to keep us focused on our chains — to fill our minds with a sense of helplessness in the face of our obstacles. As we focus on our chains, we take on the mind of a prisoner. As we constantly think about our wounds, our pain, or our addiction, we grant "the chains" greater power. The walls seem higher; the bars seem thicker.

God, however, instructs us not to focus on our past, our wounds, or our failures but to focus on who we are and what we have as citizens of the kingdom of heaven. More importantly, he invites us to focus on him as the ultimate prize of our faith. When we have him, then we have freedom. "My eyes are ever on the LORD, for only he will release my feet from the snare" (Ps. 25:15). Rather than meditating on the strength of the enemy we are to focus on the overwhelming strength of our king. Ten of the twelve spies who crossed the Jordan to "recon" the Promised Land focused on the strength of the enemy (Num. 13:33). Joshua and Caleb brought a different report. They did not deny the size of the enemy, but their focus was on the size of their God who had promised the victory. They eventually entered the land promised by God. The ten who focused on the enemy died in the wilderness. What we choose as our focus in life, will define our life.

Many believers have made brokenness their identity. These individuals focus on the past rather than the present or the future; on what God has not yet done for them rather than what he has done for them; on their lack of resources rather than the resources they have in Christ; on their weakness rather than on his strength, and; on their view of themselves rather than on his view of them. A significant part of transformation in the Kingdom of

God is based on choosing a kingdom mind-set. The gospel of the kingdom points us to power rather than weakness, abundance rather than poverty, and significance rather than insignificance. The reality of the Kingdom of God on earth enables us to choose a heavenly focus, as we become what we behold.

Paul knew about extreme "personal makeovers." He wrote, "Now the Lord is the Spirit, and where the Spirit of the Lord is, there is freedom. And we all, with unveiled face, beholding the glory of the Lord, are being changed into his likeness from one degree of glory to another; for this comes from the Lord who is the Spirit" (2 Cor. 3:17-18).

Notice that this kingdom mind-set is directly related to our freedom and our freedom is directly related to our focus. The Apostle Paul did not miss this point: "Whatever is true, whatever is noble, whatever is right, whatever is pure, whatever is lovely, whatever is admirable — if anything is excellent or praiseworthy — think about such things" (Phil. 4:8). "We fix our eyes not on what is seen, but on what is unseen" (2 Cor. 4:18). "Fix your thoughts on Jesus" (Heb. 3:1). "Let us fix our eyes on Jesus.." (Heb. 12:2).

In the natural, whenever you have five loaves and two fish to feed a crowd, you send everyone home. In the kingdom, you pray for the abundance of heaven to be manifested and feed every person in the crowd with food to spare. In the verses above, Paul tells us to fix our eyes and our thoughts on Jesus. To *fix* is to establish a permanent position that does not waiver. Our focus determines our view of reality. For those in the Kingdom of God, reality is not what is seen with the natural eyes but what is seen with the eyes of faith and the eyes of our heart. The focus we choose in our seeing, listening, speaking, and thinking will determine the lenses through which we view life.

If we focus on who we were without Christ, then even though we are in him, we will continue to live as those outside of Christ and outside of his kingdom. Our perspective will be that of a person imprisoned by our past with little hope of escape. We will live as one forgiven but believing that all the power of God to take away our pain, our shame, and our bondage is reserved for our days in heaven but not on this earth. As current citizens of heaven and children of the king, however, we are to see life and ourselves as God sees us. This view is not a denial of our need to become more like Christ, but it is actually God's strategy for shaping us into his image.

In the flesh, we continue to expect God to respond to us on the basis of our sinfulness as if he defines us and our relationship with him on the basis of our faults and failures. But Scripture says that we are clothed in the righteousness of Christ, placed in him and defined by him. We obsess on our sin. God obsesses on our righteousness and always wants to respond to us on the basis of our righteousness in Christ. That is a huge implication of the gospel of the Kingdom of God. In the kingdom, God views his children the same, whether they are walking on streets of gold or on the dusty streets of this world. He delights in both and is willing to extend the blessings of heaven to both, as we come to him with the expectation of his provision.

When our focus is on Christ — his work, his promises, our standing in heaven, the glory that is ours and will be ours, the goodness of God, the Spirit of freedom, the authority of our King, the riches that we have in him, we will become aware of our resources rather than our shortcomings, our future rather than our past, and who we are rather than who we were. We become what we behold and our freedom is found in what we have rather than in what we lack. The promises and the power of God must order our lives, rather than our weaknesses, our failings, or our past — on earth as it is in heaven.

In the end, the kingdom will fill the earth and God's heart will be expressed perfectly in every corner of that kingdom. For now, the blessings of the kingdom are available by faith and God's grace to those citizens of heaven who still dwell on the earth. We still live in enemy territory. We still battle against spiritual beings that resist the reign and the blessings of God. We still fight against our own flesh and the influence of the world. All these things hinder the reign of God, but as we surrender more and more of ourselves to him, the blessings of the kingdom may be experienced more and more in us.

These blessings, like all things in the kingdom, will come to us by faith and practice. As we begin to acknowledge who we are in Christ, our inheritance as children of God, and God's willingness to extend his blessings and power to his children, we will begin to experience the life changing power of the gospel. As you progress through this study, be confident that it is God's will for you to be free from the things that hinder your walk, your love, your joy, and your service. Be confident that Christ has done everything needed for you to walk in freedom and to maintain your walk. His kingdom has come on this earth and God wants to express his perfect will on earth in your life as it is in heaven.

Personal Reflection / Journaling:
- How have you already experienced the Kingdom of God in your life?

- Read through the scriptures listed in this chapter. Ask God to speak to you through those scriptures. Write down your insights and the thoughts God reveals to you.
- What hindrances to receiving the blessings of the kingdom do you sense in your life?
- What will you do (with God's help), to remove those hindrances?

Suggested Prayer:

Father in heaven, thank you that by the blood of Christ and the power of the resurrection, you have reestablished your kingdom on earth. Thank you that you have already granted me all the rights and privileges of a citizen of heaven and a child of the king. I pray for your Spirit of wisdom and revelation to show me who I am in Christ and what I have in Christ that I may live as you intended on this earth, knowing that the power and resources of heaven are available to me through Jesus. Give me a heart fixed on Christ and enable me to behold your glory, that I might be changed into the image of your Son. In his name I pray...Amen.

Memory Verse:

"The kingdom of God does not come with your careful observation, nor will people say, 'Here it is,' or 'There it is,' because the kingdom of God is within you." (Luke 17:20-21)

Chapter Four

WHISPERS FROM HEAVEN

And after the fire came a gentle whisper. (1 Kings 19:12)

From Genesis to Revelation, the witness of Scripture is that God reveals himself to those who seek him. He does so in a variety of ways but most often he simply speaks to men and women as a personal God, bringing them encouragement, correction or direction. As I have worked with hundreds of hurting and broken people, I have come to believe that hearing the voice of God is the shortest route to healing and radical transformation in the life of every believer. This chapter will explore the biblical foundations for hearing the voice of God in your life and offer practical approaches to hearing him. It will also give you ways to sort out God's authentic voice from the counterfeit.

The idea of hearing God makes many people (even believers) suspicious and even a little nervous. After all, more than a few psychotic individuals have done bizarre, even hideous things, declaring that God told them to do so. Numbers of modern-day prophets have declared that God had shown them the date of the Lord's return or some great catastrophe, only to see the date come and go without incident. There have always been delusional people and false prophets. Scripture tells us so. But there have also been the true prophets who heard the very Word of God and the New Testament is filled with promises that God will speak personally to his children through the Holy Spirit.

Even as Christians, many of us have been taught that in these last days, God will only speak to people through the Bible. Many churches relegate the voice of God for his children to "Bible times," or some century past and declare that since we now have the fullness of God's written revelation in Scripture, he no longer speaks to men apart from the written Word. The biblical record, however, is that through the centuries God has not only revealed his will for all men through his written Word, but that he has also revealed his specific will to individuals through many other means.

Israel received the written word at Mt. Sinai. There, through Moses, God gave the Law with all its ordinances that comprise the Pentateuch, the first five books of the Bible. These books gave detailed instructions on how to live and how to worship God. Yet, God continued to speak to his people on an individual basis through additional means: in the Tent of Meeting in the wilderness (Ex. 33:7), through his prophets and, on many occasions, through angels. At times, he spoke in an audible voice, as he did to the boy Samuel or in a still small voice as he did to Elijah. He often communicated through vivid dreams and visions and even to Balaam through the mouth of a donkey.

The New Testament records the same kind of experiences where God communicated with his people through prophets, angels, dreams, visions, the casting of lots, through his own Son and through his Holy Spirit. God's heart in this matter is very clear. God wants to speak to his people on a personal level as well as through the general revelation of his written Word and has gone to great lengths to do so.

Consider all the ways the Father has consistently revealed himself to man.

- Through his creation (Rom. 1:20; Ps. 19:1-2)
- Through his prophets (Heb. 1:1)
- Through his Son (Heb. 1:2)
- Through his written Word (2 Tim. 3:16)
- Through direct encounters (Gen. 18; Exod. 3; Exod. 33:7; 1 Sam. 3)
- Through the casting of lots (Acts 1:26)
- Through dreams and visions (Acts 2:18)
- Through circumstances (1 Sam. 14:6-12)
- Through visitations by angels (Matt. 1:20; Luke 1:11, 26; 2:13, etc.)

- Through his people to one another. (1 Cor. 14:26-33)
- Through the Holy Spirit (Jn. 16:13; Rom. 8:14,16)

The most common medium for hearing from God is, indeed, through the written Word, for God is speaking to us even then by his Spirit, as we understand and receive insights into Scripture. Paul assures us that without revelation from the Spirit, we cannot even begin to understand spiritual truths. "The man without the Spirit does not accept the things that come from the Spirit of God, for they are foolishness to him, and he cannot understand them, because they are spiritually discerned." (1 Cor. 2:14) Jesus himself promised that the Holy Spirit would "lead us into all truth" (John 16:13) and would "teach us all things" (John 14:26).

It is the Holy Spirit who teaches us, leads us into truth, and gives us understanding of spiritual things including the Bible. Even when we are seeking to know God and his will through personal reflection on the scriptures, the Holy Spirit is directing our thoughts — giving us understanding and *personal* application of his Word. In this process of illumination, God is already speaking to us apart from or in addition to his written Word as he raises thoughts and insights up into our conscious mind.

Through the Holy Spirit, God also speaks to our hearts and minds apart from our reflection on the Word. Notice the language of the following texts.

He calls his own sheep by name and leads them out...his sheep follow him because they know his voice...they do not recognize a strangers voice...I am the good shepherd; I know my sheep and my sheep know me. (John 10:3-5, 14-15)

But when he, the Spirit of truth, comes, he will guide you into all truth. He will not speak on his own; he will speak only what he hears, and he will tell you what is yet to come. (John 16:13-14)

The Spirit himself testifies with our spirit that we are God's children. (Rom. 8:16)

Notice that these verses emphasize the voice of the Spirit *speaking* and *testifying* to us. The written Word is always foundational and is the plumb line by which we judge any additional message we believe to be from God. But the

New Testament is filled with examples of people hearing God and receiving direction from him apart from the written Word.

Let me be clear at this point. I am not saying that God will give new doctrines or general revelation that is binding for the church as a whole. He will give direction and understanding to individuals, churches, and nations for specific times, needs and events apart from his Word. That is primarily the ministry of the Holy Spirit through personal revelation, prophetic gifts, words of knowledge, words of wisdom, dreams and visions, and so forth. It also continues to be the work of angels who were created as ministering spirits, sent forth to minister to God's people (Heb. 1:14). On occasion, Jesus himself will speak directly to a person as he did to Saul on the road to Damascus.

The Process of Revelation

Although God speaks to us in myriad ways, the most common way we hear from him under the New Covenant is directly through his Spirit. The Holy Spirit is the Spirit of revelation (Eph.1:17). How do we most often experience revelation? What does God sound like most of the time? Does it thunder while God shouts from heaven to give us a word? I used to think so. At least, I thought if God ever did speak to me, I would hear a voice very distinct from my own and unmistakably God. Although we may still hear the audible voice of God on occasion, have angelic visitations, or receive vivid dreams and visions, it is not the normative way most of us will hear from him. We most often hear from God as the Holy Spirit reveals God's will to us internally. The process is simple though supernatural. Many people find it helpful to know the normative process of revelation so that they may have confidence that they have heard from God.

Consider these verses:

The Spirit searches all things, even the deep things of God.... In the same way no one knows the thoughts of God except the Spirit of God. We have not received the spirit of the world but the Spirit who is from God, that we may understand what God has freely given us. (1 Cor. 2:9-13)

But when he, the Spirit of truth, comes, he will guide you into all truth...he will bring glory to me by taking from what is mine and making it known to you. (John 16:13,15)

The Spirit himself testifies with our spirit that we are God's children. (Rom. 8:16)

I keep asking that... the glorious Father, may give you the Spirit of wisdom and revelation, so that you may know him better. I pray also that the eyes of your heart may be enlightened in order that you may know the hope to which he has called you, the riches of his glorious inheritance in the saints, and his incomparably great power for us who believe. (Eph. 1:17-19)

In these verses, the revelatory work of the Holy Spirit is emphasized. Paul is clear that the spirit of a man knows the deepest thoughts of a man. In the same way, the Holy Spirit searches the mind of God, even the deep things. The Spirit of God then takes the thoughts of the Father and the Son and makes them known to us by testifying (speaking truth) to our spirits. In the context of revelation, it is the idea of the eyes or understanding of our hearts being opened. As the Spirit speaks to our spirit, and gives interpretation or enlightenment, then these thoughts rise up into our heart and into our conscious mind so that we can hear, sense or see what God is showing us.

We often miss the voice of God because we expect it to sound like someone else's voice speaking to us as something internally or externally audible. God does speak like that at times, but usually his word comes to us as a thought, which may feel or sound much like our own thoughts. The Word of God is simply being made known to us through our conscious mind, though it began as a thought in the mind of God. His word may come as a clear, spontaneous thought or dialogue or it may simply be one word that is impressed upon you. It may be a picture or image that rises up in your conscious thought or a feeling, a sense, or an impression about something. It may also come as a dream or a vision.

Testing the Spirits

Most often, we will hear God's voice as our own thoughts. Usually a thought, impression, or dream has a quality to it that alerts us that the Spirit is speaking, but it takes time to learn what is from God and what is from another source. Sometimes, we are left with the dilemma of determining if we have just heard from God, merely from our own storehouse of thoughts, or from the enemy. When someone else brings a "word of God" to us as a prophetic word or word of knowledge we may face the same dilemma. We must then test what we have heard. "Dear friends, do not believe every spirit, but test the spirits to see whether they are from God" (1 John 4:1).

The primary test for determining whose voice we have heard is always the Word of God. We must determine whether or not the thought, impression or interpretation is consistent with biblical truth. God will never contradict himself. If it is not in line with the written Word, disregard what you have heard. Of course, that also places a burden on us to know the Word of God well enough to test what we have heard against it.

There are other tests in addition to the written Word of God that you will want to apply to the things you have heard.

1. Does the "voice" or message seem consistent with the character of God or Jesus?

Many of us are unsure about the character of God or mistakenly project the temperament of our own fathers onto our heavenly Father. The character of Christ may be discovered in the gospels and the character of God is succinctly revealed both in the fruit of the Spirit passages (Gal. 5:22-23) and in Paul's description of love, since God is love (1 Cor. 13:4-8). If the "voice" you hear is accusing, condemning, rude, boastful, mean, angry, or demeaning, it is not from God. If the voice asks you to do something contrary to the scriptures or of it violates his righteousness, it is not from God.

2. Does the message produce peace in your heart?

Jesus said, "Peace I leave with you" (John 14:27). Sometimes, God speaks things we don't fully understand. He may send conviction (not condemnation) about sin in our life, speak a word of discipline, send a message about coming changes, or even warn us of hardships we will face. When God has finished speaking, there is nearly always a sense of peace that surrounds his word because his goal is always to help us, not to hurt us.

3. Do spiritual mentors sense that what you have heard is from God?

It is always valuable to have one or two spiritual mentors around you who have learned to hear God's voice themselves so that you may share with them what you are hearing. They will often have a sense about the quality and content of what you are hearing that will help you develop your own discernment.

Discerning the Source

In general, we will need to discern the difference between things we hear from God and things we hear from our own flesh or from the enemy. The summaries that follow offer more indicators of whose voice you have heard by the qualities of the thought or impression you have received and the fruit it bears in your heart.

God the Father, God the Son, and God the Holy Spirit come as the good shepherd (see John 15).

It is God's nature to love and draw you to him. He is a comforter, an encourager and a teller of truth...always speaking the truth in love. He tends to give clear, specific instructions when directing you. He points you to Jesus and righteousness. He is kind and quick to forgive. He draws glory to himself because it is in your best interest. He delights in you and wants to impart hope in every circumstance. He never compares you to others or shames you for your past.

Satan is a liar, the tempter and the accuser of the brethren who comes to kill, steal and destroy.

He intimidates, discourages, demands and threatens. He accuses God and argues against the Word of God. He condemns, accuses and assaults your sense of worth. He brings up past failures and resurrects shame. He plants fear. He appeals to your pride and sense of entitlement to justify sin in your life. He plays to your sense of victimization. He points you away from Jesus.

The flesh or natural man is self-focused.

The flesh is "all about me." It demands its own rights and privileges. It always defends itself and rationalizes its actions. It exalts its intellect over the Word of God. It is self-promoting. The natural man in us pushes for control and uses manipulation to get what he wants. The natural man always feels entitled and is quick to take offense. The flesh depends on self and personal resources rather than God. The natural man is quick to pursue desires of the flesh.

Spontaneity

Another good test is the spontaneity of the thought, impression, or vision. Jesus said that the Spirit would be like a spring of living water welling up inside of us. Often there is a refreshing flow of thoughts, impressions or pictures you did not generate by thinking through an issue. Often it is a thought you never considered before, or one that you know would not have come out of your natural man.

As you hear a voice, you may want to look at these summaries to help you identify the source. In reality, Satan and the natural man seem very much alike. The best way to identify any counterfeit is to intimately know the authentic. Know the heart and Word of God and you won't go wrong.

These are tests to help you learn to discern the spoken word of God in your life. As in learning any new language or skill, you will become more proficient with time and practice. Before making important decisions based on a word or dream, it is wise to always get confirmation through spiritual mentors and intercessors, even when you are experienced at hearing the Shepherd's voice. You may also simply ask Jesus if what you heard is from him. If it is not, he will tell you.

Sometimes, committed believers don't want to hear God because they are afraid of being deceived. Jesus promised that the Holy Spirit will lead us into all truth and remind us of all the things that Jesus has already taught us (John 14:26). If we sincerely ask Jesus to keep us from error and to teach us to hear only his voice, I believe he can be trusted to show us if we are getting off track.

Learning to hear the voice of God is a process of trial and error. You will make mistakes and, at times, feel foolish. There is a cost to developing intimacy with God but hearing him is essential to healing and freedom as he tells you the truth about your past, your wounds and his love for you. Jesus promised that his truth would set us free. I have seen it do so hundreds of times as Jesus spoke his truth over the lies of the enemy, breaking those strongholds as soon as he spoke.

Being an Effective Receiver

Sometimes God intrudes into our lives with a life-shaking word as he did with Saul on his way to Damascus (Acts 9). Sometimes he calls out to us in the middle of the night as he did to Samuel (1 Sam. 3). But most often, his is the "still, quiet voice" of Elijah's cave (1 Kings19: 11-12). Our part is to become effective receivers. The voice of God fills the air like radio waves, but if we are to hear his voice, we must be tuned to the right frequency. The following guidelines help us "tune in" to God.

Guidelines for Hearing God

Expect to hear from God. (John 16:12-15)
Jesus promised he would send his Spirit to teach us, remind us, lead us, and to speak to us. Expect what Jesus promised.

Be willing to hear from God about every area of your life. (2 Cor. 10:5)
If you want to restrict God's involvement in your life by declaring certain areas "off limits," you will not hear from him often. Those will be the areas about which he wants to speak most often, since those areas will be the very strongholds in your life that keep you in bondage.

Invite him to speak. (1 Sam. 3:8-9)
Literally ask Jesus to speak to you and invite him to say whatever he wants. A direct invitation opens the door of communication.

Be still and know.... (Ps. 46:10)
Stop your busyness. Learn to sit and listen quietly.

Be patient. (Ps. 130:5)
Often, you will need to wait on the Lord, sitting quietly for a while. God may also choose not to say anything that day. Keep asking and listening.

Enter his presence with worship, the Word, thanksgiving and prayer. (Ps. 100:4)
The psalmist tells us that praise brings us into God's presence. Seeking God through praise, his Word, and thanksgiving before listening prepares you to hear more clearly.

Write down what you hear, see or feel. (Hab. 2:1-2)
God's Word is precious. Journaling is an effective way to remember what God has spoken to you personally. Review your journal from time to time and see how his hand has been on your life.

Act on the things you believe you have heard from God. (John 14:21)
Sometimes God will speak things that are just to be received rather than acted upon. But when he tells you to do anything, you should act. Obedience brings

greater revelation. Disobedience quenches the Spirit and hinders your ability to hear from God. On major decisions, seek confirmation through prayer and spiritual mentors before moving ahead.

If you sense that the enemy is interfering with your ability to hear God, before you begin to listen for his voice, make declarations to exercise the authority you have in Christ.
Suggested declaration:

"In the name of Jesus and according to the Word of God, I declare that I have the mind of Christ. I now submit my intellect, my emotions, my will, and my imagination to Jesus and ask him to capture every thought and make it his. In his name, by his blood, and by his authority, I bind Satan and any demonic spirit from speaking to me. In the name of Jesus, I command you to be silent and not to interfere in any way while the Lord Jesus speaks to me...Amen.

Exercise in Hearing:
Have a pen and paper ready. Spend a few minutes praising God and giving him thanks. You may do so with singing, a prayer of praise, or by reading scriptures out loud that express praise to the Lord. You may want to play your favorite worship CD and join in with it.

Now pray...

Lord Jesus, I believe you want to speak to me. Lord, tune my heart that I might hear your voice. Jesus, give me your spirit of wisdom and revelation so that I might know you better and open the eyes of my heart that I might see those things you would show me. In the name of Jesus, I bind Satan and every demonic spirit and command them to be silent as my Lord speaks. Lord Jesus, will you speak to me now? Will you tell me how you feel about me or what you want most for me at this time in my life? Lord Jesus, I ask this in your name.

Listen quietly with your mind at rest. Simply listen with your heart and write down what you hear, what you see, or what you feel. Do not try to make it happen. Wait on the Lord.

After listening for his response, continue to pray...

*Lord Jesus, what do **you** want me to pray about at this time?*

Let your mind be at rest. Do not try to think of prayer needs or a prayer focus. Simply shift your thinking into neutral and wait on the Lord to bring something to your mind. Pray for whatever or whoever comes to mind.

If you are not sure if you heard anything from the Lord, do not be discouraged. This is practice and you are learning to listen with your heart. Continue to ask Jesus daily to speak to you about these matters. In time you will hear. God desires to speak to you and will. You may also ask him if there is anything you are unaware of that is hindering your communication with him.

Hindrances to Hearing God

Sometimes we may find it hard to hear the Lord even though we are asking and listening. The following issues may create a barrier to hearing. Ask God to highlight any of these areas you need to deal with so you can open up to the flow of his Spirit in you.

Religious Preconceptions

One of the great hindrances to the work of God in our lives is the preconceptions we carry from being taught about God by people who have had limited experience with God. Knowing doctrine is not the same as knowing the one who authored the doctrine. Be open to God's fresh work in your life and take a fresh look at Scripture. Be careful not to miss or turn down God's move in your life because he isn't operating according to your set expectations or the expectation of those who taught you.

Working Rather Than Seeking

Sometimes we get caught up in being busy for God rather than in seeking God himself. For many of us, especially men, doing is much easier than relating. It is ironic that many of us are so busy serving God that we rarely find time just to sit with God and listen. Servants only work for the master. Sons and daughters sit in his presence. Pursue daily time with God even if you begin with just a few minutes. Abandon the shopping list approach to prayer and spend some time each day just asking God to speak to you about his heart, a scripture, or a thought and just listen.

An Unresponsive Heart

"So, as the Holy Spirit says: 'Today, if you hear his voice, do not harden your hearts.'" (Heb. 3:8)

Hardened hearts do not make good receivers. Many of us have been deeply wounded by life. As a result, we have developed extensive defense mechanisms to guard ourselves from being wounded again. We are rarely open and vulnerable even with those closest to us. We still keep our deepest fears, hopes, and feelings to ourselves because we continue to fear rejection.

Too often, we view God with the same suspicion and distrust. If your heart has been hardened by life so that you are guarded, distrustful or controlling, ask God to break down those strongholds and give you a softened and responsive heart to his love and his Word. God is aware of your brokenness and your fear and is willing to heal those hurts. Talk to him about it.

Un-repented Sin

"If I had cherished sin in my heart, the Lord would not have listened." (Ps. 66:18)

David was aware of the fact that if we love sin more than God, it will limit our relationship with him. Take an inventory. If there is a persistent sin you love, excuse or justify, acknowledge it and submit that sin to the cross. David was also aware that we are often blind to our own failings. Because of that, David invited God to perform a spiritual MRI. "Search me, O God, and know my heart; test me and know my anxious thoughts. See if there is any offensive way in me, and lead me in the way everlasting." (Ps. 139:23-24). To maintain an open channel to God, surrender all your sin, known and unknown, to the cross of Christ.

Unforgiveness

"For if you forgive men when they sin against you, your heavenly Father will also forgive you. But if you do not forgive men their sins, your Father will not forgive your sins." (Matt. 6:14-15)

God simply says that an open relationship with him depends on our willingness to forgive others as he has forgiven us. Choose to forgive those who have wounded you. The spirit of forgiveness in the kingdom was demonstrated on the cross when Jesus asked the Father to forgive those who had crucified him although there was no repentance in their hearts. Biblical forgiveness is a decision to no longer require payment for a wrong done to you and to turn judgment over to God. It is a decision of the will to no longer act in ways that make others pay for what they have done. Forgiving those who have wronged you, praying for them and blessing them does not excuse them. God is a righteous judge and will deal with their sins. Forgiveness aligns your heart with the heart of Christ and keeps your heart from being closed by bitterness and resentment. Unforgiveness creates a huge barrier in your relationship with the Father.

Half-hearted Faith, Double-Mindedness

"But when he asks, he must believe and not doubt, because he who doubts is like a wave of the sea, blown and tossed by the wind. That man should not think he will receive anything from the Lord; he is a double-minded man, unstable in all he does." (James 1:6-8)

When we try to serve two masters — God and whatever else we love — we will not often hear his voice. God is a God who must be first and the only "god" in our lives. When we try to live with one foot in the world and one foot in the kingdom, we must push back against the Spirit who is always calling us to God. To do so dulls our "spiritual hearing." Pursue God. Ask him sincerely to give you an undivided heart set wholly on Jesus. "Then you will call upon me and come and pray to me, and I will listen to you. You will seek me and find me when you seek me with all your heart." (Jer. 29:12-13)

The Enemy

"Put on the full armor of God so that you can take your stand against the devil's schemes." (Eph. 6:11)

Satan schemes against you. His goal is to hinder your relationship with God and to make you ineffective as a believer. He will intervene in your attempt to hear God with distractions, random thoughts, memories that dredge up grief and shame designed to make you feel as if God had no interest in speaking with you. As you begin to be still and listen for God's voice, you may want to bind the voice of Satan by the blood and the authority of Jesus we suggested earlier.

Personal Reflection / Journaling:

Reflect on the *Guidelines for Hearing God* and the *Hindrances to Hearing God* listed earlier in this chapter. What is God "highlighting" for you in those guidelines? Is there anything you need to confess, repent of and submit to the lordship of Christ?

Reflect on the following passages each day, until you desire and expect to hear from God through his Spirit. Write down your thoughts about these verses and anything you believe God is revealing to you personally through these passages.

> He calls his own sheep by name and leads them out…his sheep follow him because they know his voice…they do not recognize a strangers voice…I am the good shepherd; I know my sheep and my sheep know me. (John 10:3-5, 14-15)

> But when he, the Spirit of truth, comes, he will guide you into all truth. He will not speak on his own; he will speak only what he hears, and he will tell you what is yet to come. (John 16:13-14)

> The Spirit himself testifies with our spirit that we are God's children. (Rom. 8:16)

Suggested Prayer Process:

As you begin to pray, ask God to give you "ears to hear" his Spirit and "eyes to see" what he might show you. Ask him to reveal anything in your life, your attitudes, or your beliefs that hinder you from hearing his voice. Ask him to give you a responsive heart to his word…written or spoken.

- Begin with praise and thanksgiving.
- Pray for others.
- Pray for the advance of God's kingdom on the earth.
- Pray for your own heart and your own needs.
- Ask God to speak to you about anything he wants you to know.

- Sit quietly and listen. If you sense that the enemy is disrupting the process, bind him to silence by the name, the blood and the authority of Jesus.
- Write down anything you believe Jesus is saying to you.

Evaluate what you heard.
- Is it consistent with the Word of God?
- Does it reflect the character of God?
- Did it create peace in your heart?
- Do you need to take action on anything God spoke to you?
- Share what you have heard with spiritual mentors.

Memory Verse:
"Today, if you hear his voice, do not harden your hearts." (Hebrews 4:7)

Chapter Five

WHEN EVERYTHING CHANGED

For the message of the cross is foolishness to those who are perishing, but to us who are being saved it is the power of God. (1 Cor. 1:18)

The cross, as it embodies the suffering and death of Jesus Christ for our sins, is the central message of the New Testament. This sacrifice offered by Christ himself answered the legal claims of the Law on each of us and literally broke the power of sin in our lives. By his blood, Jesus ransomed us from the dominion of darkness and gave us life in the Kingdom of God. An incredible shift took place in the courts of heaven as Jesus died on the cross, opening the door to our amazing inheritance in Christ. Part of that inheritance is healing and freedom. This chapter explores the great exchange that took place on the cross so that, by faith, we can stand firmly against the accusing and condemning thoughts of the enemy. Our enemy constantly tries to use our past failures and present weaknesses to steal our transformation and freedom.

The Messianic Ministry of Jesus

There are numerous prophetic passages in the Old Testament that point to the coming of the anointed one of Israel who would free Israel from oppression and establish an eternal throne of righteousness for the nation. Jesus came to fulfill those divine promises. Underlying the fulfillment of those promises was his sacrificial death on a cross.

There were two parts to the Messianic mission. The second part was to come in power to set Israel free from her oppressors and to fully establish God's eternal kingdom on earth. The Jews were waiting for that with great anticipation in the days of Jesus. The first part, which Jewish scholars had missed and which was almost inconceivable to any Jew, was for the Messiah to pay the penalty for their sins by his suffering and death.

For centuries, the extensive system of temple sacrifices pointed to two essential truths. First of all, to pay for man's rebellion and sin, blood had to be shed. Sin is rebellion and rebellion is a capital crime. Secondly, the temple sacrifices pointed to the amazing grace of God. The sacrifices embodied a prophetic truth that God was willing to accept a substitute for the death owed by every sinner. Through the sacrifice of an innocent substitute the demands of God's holiness would be satisfied. It was at the cross that Jesus did for us what we could never do for ourselves. It was a moment during which the sinless Lamb of God took on the penalty for our sin: "God made him who had no sin to be sin for us, so that in him we might become the righteousness of God" (2 Cor. 5:21).

The first Adam, seduced by the tempter, had incurred multiple curses for himself and all his descendants: separation from the presence of God, physical deterioration and death, disease, and the world's ecosystems thrown out of balance. God had placed the earth under Adam's dominion. As he came into agreement with Satan, he became subject to Satan, and so did the world that was under Adam's command. Satan then became the "prince of this world" (John 12:31).

Jesus, the second Adam, came to face the enemy again as a champion for the human race. Jesus came as Adam the first time. He came fully in the flesh but without the fallen nature of man because he was fathered by the Holy Spirit. He, like Adam, had the capacity to sin and was tempted in every way that we are. However, unlike Adam, Jesus did not submit to Satan but submitted perfectly to his heavenly Father.

Jesus, although he was fully God, did not exercise his divine attributes while in the flesh on this earth. He came fully as man, as Adam was before "the Fall," having man's intended authority over the created realm. His miracles were expressions of his God-given authority and the power of God that flowed through him because he was perfectly aligned with the Father's will. Jesus came to win back what had been lost in the Garden of Eden. He came not only to demonstrate that man, before the Fall, was indeed capable of resisting the devil's taunts and temptations, but also to pay the price himself for all who had been handed over to the enemy through Adam.

On the cross he disarmed Satan. He severed the legal claims of sin on the life of every believer born-again as a descendent of the second Adam, Jesus Christ. Just as Adam's sin and the consequences were passed down to his descendants, so the righteousness of Christ was passed down to all who would believe in him. As the curses assigned to Adam were passed down through the generations of his seed, so the blessings of the Kingdom of God were made available to the spiritual descendants of Jesus.

The Great Exchange

An amazing exchange took place on the cross. Christ took on our sin and all its attachments: guilt, shame, poverty, separation from the presence of the Father, and the curse of the Law. We took on his standing with the Father as those totally without sin (2 Cor. 5:21; Rom. 6:23; Gal. 3:13-14).

An all-encompassing exchange has **literally** taken place in the spiritual realm. Because of this *exchange*, we are able to approach the throne of grace with confidence, knowing that God's help and mercy will be available to us (Heb. 4:16). As we approach God, asking him to set us free from those things that hinder our life in Christ, we can fully expect his help. Because of Jesus, we are no longer cursed, alienated sinners opposed to God. Instead, we stand before him as his children **with all the blessings of heaven available to us. You do not have to persuade God, buy God, nag God, or coerce God to hear your prayers to set you free. He is willing. It is why Jesus came. The cross has made you a welcomed son or daughter in the throne room of God.**

By faith in what Jesus did for us, we *literally* have moved from a position of ...

Sin to Righteousness. "God made him who had no sin to be sin for us, so that in him we might become the righteousness of God." (2 Cor. 5:21)

Alienation to Adoption. "In love he predestined us to be adopted as his sons through Jesus Christ, in accordance with his pleasure and will..." (Eph. 1:4-5)

Slavery to Sonship. "Because you are sons, God sent the Spirit of his Son into our hearts, the Spirit who calls out 'Abba, Father.' So you are no longer a slave, but a son." (Gal. 4:6-7)

Death to Life. "As for you, you were dead in your transgressions and sins, in which you used to live… But because of his great love for us, God, who is rich in mercy, made us alive with Christ." (Eph. 2:1-2, 4-5)

Rejection to Acceptance. "Accept one another, then, just as Christ accepted you, in order to bring praise to God." (Rom. 15:7)

Poverty to Riches. "For you know the grace of our Lord Jesus Christ, that though he was rich, yet for your sakes he became poor, so that you through his poverty might become rich." (2 Cor. 8:9)

Darkness to Light. "For you were once darkness, but now you are light in the Lord." (Eph. 5:8)

Alienation to Citizenship. "Remember that at that time you were separate from Christ, excluded from citizenship in Israel and foreigners to the covenants of the promise, without hope and without God in the world…you are no longer foreigners and aliens, but fellow citizens with God's people." (Eph. 2:12, 19)

Fear to Confidence. "Let us then approach the throne of grace with confidence, so that we may receive mercy and find grace to help us in our time of need." (Heb. 4:16)

Old to New. "Therefore, if anyone is in Christ, he is a new creation; the old has gone the new has come!" (2 Cor. 5:17)

Cursed to Blessed. "Christ redeemed us from the curse of the law by becoming a curse for us." (Gal. 3:13)

Bondage to Freedom. "he has sent me to proclaim freedom for the prisoners." (Luke 4:18)

Condemned to Justified. "Therefore, there is now no condemnation for those who are in Christ Jesus, because through Christ Jesus the law of the Spirit of life set me free from the law of sin and death." (Rom. 8:1-2)

Weak to Strong. "I can do everything through him who gives me strength." (Phil. 4:13)

Ruled to Ruling. "You were dead in your transgressions and sins, in which you used to live when you followed the ways of this world and of the ruler of the kingdom of the air ... And God raised us up with Christ and seated us with him in the heavenly realms…" (Eph. 2:1-2, 6)

Declaring What Christ Has Done for Us

"That if you confess with your mouth, 'Jesus is Lord,' and believe in your heart that God raised him from the dead, you will be saved." (Rom. 10:9) There is a connection between confessing or declaring with our mouths and believing in our hearts. I may believe that something is true on an intellectual level but until it penetrates my heart (my emotions, my will, and my core beliefs) very little changes.

God has created us in a way that makes our verbal expression of a truth sink deeper into our souls, producing greater faith in our hearts. Confessing or declaring God's truths will deepen and personalize our belief in these truths which will then change our perspectives, our emotions, and our decisions based on God's Word.

In the spiritual realm, these declarations help keep us aligned with Christ and deepen our faith. Faith is our shield against the assaults of the enemy. In Revelation 12, John tells us that the brethren overcame Satan by the blood of the Lamb and the word of their testimony. Verbal confession and declaration of God's truth and what he has done for you are powerful weapons to be used to resist the enemy.

A great beginning place is to agree with God about who we are in Christ. I encourage you to confess out loud the declarations that follow each day for the next thirty days. Doing so will enable the Holy Spirit to write God's truth over those broken places of belief about who you are. Believing who you are in Christ is absolutely essential to finding freedom!

Declaration of Faith—My Identity in Christ

In the name of Jesus and by his blood …

I renounce the lies of Satan and his accusations that come against me. I renounce the lies that I am bound up in my brokenness, weak, worthless, and displeasing to my Heavenly Father. I renounce shame, worthlessness, inadequacy, rejection, guilt, accusation and condemnation because in Jesus Christ I am totally loved, totally forgiven, totally accepted, totally valued, and totally competent.

In the name of Jesus and according to the Word of God, I now declare that …
I am a child of God. (John 1:12)

I did not choose God but he chose me and has made me a personal friend of Jesus Christ. (John 15:5)

I have been declared innocent of all sin by the blood of Christ. (Rom. 5:1)

1 am joined with Christ and his Spirit and I am made holy by that union. (1 Cor. 6:17)

I have been fully ransomed from the evil one at an incredible price and belong totally to Christ. (1 Cor. 6:19, 20)

I am a member of the Body of Christ, designed by God, gifted by God, and placed exactly where he wants me. I have a destiny in Christ that God has begun in me and will see to completion. (1 Cor. 12:27; Ps. 139:13,16; Eph. 2:10; 1 Cor. 12:18; Phil. 1:6)

I am a saint, a holy one of God. (Eph. 1:1)

I have been adopted by God, chosen by Jesus Christ, and am a priest and a member of God's royal family. I possess all the rights and privileges of a citizen of heaven. (Eph. 1:5; John 15:16; Eph. 2:19; 1 Peter 2:9)

I lack nothing for godliness and love because I have been made complete in Jesus Christ. (Col. 2:10)

I am free forever from all condemnation and any condemnation is a lie from the evil one. (Rom. 8:1)

I am totally united to the love of God in Christ Jesus and nothing can separate me from that love. (Rom 8:35-39)

Because I am a child of God, washed in the blood of Jesus, I can come before the throne of grace at any time with boldness and a full expectation of help in time of need. (Heb. 4:16)

I am a man/woman of God who stands firm in Christ, anointed by God, sealed by the king, filled by his Spirit and guaranteed the blessings of God, which are to come. (2 Cor. 1:21-22)

I have not been given a spirit of fear but of power and love and self-control. (1 Tim 1:7)

I am a branch of the true vine, Jesus Christ. His power, love and grace flow into me, through me and into the world. (John 15:1, 5)

I am a minister of reconciliation made competent to serve by the Spirit and power of God. (2 Cor. 3:6; 5:17-21)

Because I am in Christ, I am a new creation, a servant of righteousness, and free from the power of sin. (2 Cor. 5:17)

In everything, I am more than a conqueror though Jesus Christ. (Rom. 8:37)

Because I am loved and treasured, God is for me — so no one can stand against me. (Rom 8:31)

I am not an orphan and I am never alone because God has said, "No matter what, I will never leave you, I will never forsake you." (Heb. 13:5)

Through all these things God, who cannot lie, declares that I am absolutely loved, totally accepted, worthy in Christ, a treasured son/daughter in the household of

God, personally chosen by Jesus Christ, holy and destined for greatness in him. I say what God says.

In the name of Jesus, I renounce all lies to the contrary and in his name and by his blood, renounce and nullify all curses and judgments that have been spoken against me contrary to God's declared truth. Holy Spirit, write these truths on my heart today, in Jesus' name...Amen.

Position and Condition

If you are like me, in spite of hearing that Christ has made you the righteousness of God, that you are welcome in the throne room of the creator of the universe, and that all of heaven's resources are available to you, some days you may think: "Well, it doesn't feel that way to me." One of our faith difficulties is looking at ourselves and not *feeling* righteous, victorious, blessed, holy, or acceptable — only some of the words used to describe followers of Jesus in Scripture.

When we think about our condition, we feel as if there is a great chasm that separates our reality from the Word of God. We begin to think that all those words describe mature, "saintly" Christians, but not us. Satan capitalizes on those feelings to keep us from pressing into God with the confidence of beloved children. Those feelings can cause us to keep our distance from the Father, believing that we are still somehow unacceptable to him.

Here is the good news: In the mind of God, we are already those things, while we are not yet those things. In Christ, God gives us the **position** of being righteous while his Spirit works on our **condition** of weakness. The writer of Hebrews says it this way. "By one sacrifice he has made perfect forever those who are being made holy" (Heb. 10:14).

Notice that we **have been** made perfect forever (position) while we are **being made holy** (condition). God declares "righteousness" to be your legal standing before him while he is shaping you into the image of his Son. Your position is established by an event (your faith in Jesus Christ). Transforming your condition is a process.

Here is the amazing thing. We see ourselves as we are today or as we were in the past. God sees us as we will be. Our God is a God "who calls things that are not as though they were" (Rom. 4:17). He can do this because he will certainly bring to pass the things he calls out. He has called out our position and will bring our condition in line with it.

God is a builder. Jesus was a carpenter. God doesn't despise our condition because he sees the end from the beginning. Think about building a house. Plans are drawn up in detail, drawings of the house are rendered by the architects, colors are chosen, counter tops, plumbing fixtures — everything is planned and the final product is clearly pictured by those building the house. It is the buyer's dream house and they know the end from the beginning.

At first the house won't look like much. Dirt in a field full of weeds, a little trash, and red ants will likely be the first scene. Then there will be ditches and piles of dirt followed by concrete and roughed-in plumbing, pieces of white plastic pipe sticking out of a concrete slab going nowhere. Then there will be lumber stacked next to the foundation. At that point, there is nothing beautiful or elegant about the house. Dirt, rocks, sticks and plastic pipe — not much considering the money that is going into the project. After that comes framing, wiring, and plain dry wall without color. Often, it will look chaotic and sometimes it will just look like a big mess. There will be delays. All in all, frustration will be part of the journey.

The wise builder never despises the process. He knows that each part is essential to the final product and he knows the end from the beginning. He knows that in the end, a beautiful home will stand on a once barren lot and house a family full of love and joy. God sees each of us in that way. We may at times despise the process or just see a big mess when we look at our lives, but God sees the finished product. When God looks at us, that is what he sees and that is what he values.

The Word of God speaks our final condition over us: righteous, saint, redeemed, beloved, victorious, conquering, friends, royalty and more. Each of these terms is prophetic and embodies our destiny in Christ. When God speaks it over us he calls it out. When we speak his evaluation over one another and over ourselves, we call it out. It is our eternal position in Christ. God, the master builder does not focus on our current condition, as we tend to do.

Therefore, we should learn to define ourselves by our position rather than by our condition. "We are God's workmanship, created in Christ Jesus to do good works, which God prepared in advance for us to do" (Eph. 2:10). "He that began a good work in you will carry it on to completion until the day of Jesus Christ" (Phil. 1:6). Agreeing with God about who I am in Christ is a divine weapon that severs me from my past and allows God to shape me for my future, when my condition will fully match my position.

Personal Reflection / Journaling:

Each day, read the declarations of who you are in Christ based on the exchange Christ made with you.

Ask God to speak to you about what it means to receive and live out the standing and blessings that are yours in him. Reflect on the following questions and ask God to give you a revelation of truth concerning these things.

- What does it mean for you to be "the righteousness of God"?
- What do "riches in Christ" look like in your life?
- What blessings does citizenship in heaven give you a right to receive now? Later?
- How have you already experienced being a new creation in Christ?
- For you, what does it mean to rule with Christ now?
- How should a "son" or "daughter" of the King of Glory live in this world?

Suggested Prayer Focus: Ask God to write these truths on your heart so that, by faith, you can come to walk in the blessings that have been purchased for you by his own Son. These blessings are the right of each citizen of heaven and the inheritance of every child of God. We receive them and experience them by faith. Pray daily for the Spirit of wisdom and revelation so that "the eyes of your heart may be enlightened in order that you may know the hope to which he has called you, the riches of his glorious inheritance in the saints, and his incomparably great power for us who believe" (Eph. 1:18-19).

Memory Verse:

"Therefore, if anyone is in Christ, he is a new creation; the old has gone, the new has come!" (2 Cor. 5:17)

Chapter Six

GOD'S CRAFTSMANSHIP

For we are God's workmanship created in Christ Jesus.... (Eph. 2:10)

God is in the Business of Change

The Bible is not only the story of the coming of the Messiah, but also a chronicle of God's work in transforming his people. It is his specialty. Abraham, Sarah, Isaac, Jacob, Joseph, Moses, Rahab, David, Gideon, Peter, James, John, Mary Magdalene, Saul of Tarsus — a collection of the weak, the broken, the on the run, the self-centered, the headstrong, the sinful, the demon oppressed, the unremarkable, and the reluctant — all renovated into remarkable men and women of faith who changed their world. Knowing the processes and tools that God uses to change us enables us to engage with him in his process of reconstruction rather than pushing back or missing his work in our lives. In this chapter we will examine many of those tools and processes which Paul called *divine weapons* (2 Cor. 10:4)

If you want to reflect on "the transformed," look at the lives of those listed in Hebrews 11. Each began as highly questionable candidates. Each finished in God's roll call of the greats. He wants to do the same for you. Transformation is a kingdom expectation. We are commanded to "be transformed by the renewing of your mind" (Rom. 12:2). The word "transformed" in this passage is from the Greek word "*metamorpho.*" It is the root of metamorphosis — the caterpillar to butterfly phenomena. It is the word that describes Christ when his total appearance changed on the Mount of Transfiguration as he met with Moses and Elijah, shortly before the suffering and death he was facing. The text says, "There he was transfigured before them. His face shone like the sun and his clothes became as white as the light" (Matt. 17:1-3). In that moment, Jesus was radically altered from an earthy identity to a heavenly identity. God wants us to do the same in each of us.

The New Testament calls us to be born again, to be made new, to be transformed, to be raised to walk in newness of life, and more. God isn't interested in cosmetic upgrades. He wants transformation, "spiritual metamorphosis" for every believer. Only then can we begin to fully experience the kingdom of heaven and only then can we walk in true freedom.

Power to Change

We are all called to change, but we all know how difficult real change can be. The Apostle Paul shares his own struggle in Romans 7. There he describes the relationship between our flesh and our spirit as a war. He cries out in frustration as he describes the moments when he found himself doing the very things he did not want to do and refraining from those things he truly wanted to do in his heart. He recognized that as a believer he had become a "spiritual man" who loved God and his ways but that his "natural man" or "the flesh" was still there as well and always resisted the Spirit while demanding its own way. Paul was also aware that spiritual forces push back against the work of God in our lives and reminds us that, "our struggle is not against flesh and blood, but against the rulers, against the authorities, against the powers of this dark world and against the spiritual forces of evil in the heavenly realms" (Eph. 6:12).

But, rather than throwing his hands up in defeat, he declared that although we are weak in our own strength, there is supernatural power on our side to overcome the flesh, the world, and satanic forces. "The weapons we fight with are not the weapons of the world. On the contrary, they have divine power to demolish strongholds. We demolish arguments and every pretension that sets itself up against the knowledge of God, and we take captive every thought to make it obedient to Christ." (2 Cor. 10:4-5)

These verses confirm that all the change agents of the world, based on worldly wisdom and methodology, are insufficient to truly set us free from the things that hinder our freedom. The true obstacles are strongholds within us that crumble only when divine weapons are turned against them. Only divine weapons can touch the spiritual forces arrayed against us or move the spiritual forces that would fight on our behalf. Only divine weapons will bring about the depth of change needed within each of us to be transformed, as the Father wants us to be. Anything else falls short.

Tearing Down Strongholds

When the Apostle Paul spoke of *divine weapons*, he said that they had power to demolish or tear down *strongholds*. *He* goes on to say that with God's power we demolish *arguments* and *pretensions* that set themselves up against the *knowledge* of God. He then counsels us to take our *thoughts* captive, submitting them wholly to Christ. Paul's emphasis in this passage is on our thought life. Somewhere deep within us lay powerful belief systems. Some are aligned with God's truth and others are contrary to God's truth. These belief systems shape the way we perceive reality. They are about the stuff that life is made of. Is there a God? What is he like? Can God be trusted? Does he care about me? Who am I? Do I matter? Why do I exist?

These beliefs and many others are usually established through life experiences. We will discuss the issue of core beliefs later, but for now it is enough to say that the strongholds Paul speaks about are belief systems deep within us that are contrary to God's truth. Satan works to establish and reinforce beliefs that are not aligned with God. Notice that these strongholds are active — arguing against God's revealed truth and making arrogant, deceptive claims (pretension) that deny the sovereignty and the goodness of God. God's divine weapons have power to demolish these long held beliefs and to bring them into a surrendered relationship to Jesus, who is truth. Again, I want to emphasize that secular tools and techniques for interior alteration and healing, by their very nature, fall short of tearing down strongholds that limit our ability to fully experience God. It takes spiritual power to penetrate spiritual fortifications. Paul clearly states that our real battles are not fought against flesh and blood but waged in the spiritual realm, with God's power and his weapons.

The Lie

Satan's foundational strategy against God's people is the lie. Jesus spoke of Satan and said, "there is no truth in him…he is a liar and the father of lies"

(John 8:44). He unveiled his strategy in the Garden as he subtly suggested to Adam and Eve that God was not to be trusted, that he was withholding good things from them, and did not love them as he claimed. Once Eve believed the lie, she took and ate. Adam joined her in her agreement with Satan and all was lost. Satan continues to exercise this primary strategy in the hearts and minds of believers.

In my experience, Satan constantly whispers a myriad of lies about the character of God and about my relationship with him: "God can't be trusted. He will abandon you when you need him most. You're on your own in this world. You better take care of yourself because no one else will. When did God ever answer your prayers? Not even God can love you. God only keeps his promises some of the time and only to a few of his favorites," and so on. Recognize any of those thoughts? Satan's lies fall within two frameworks. He either argues that God is not who he claims to be or that God is good and mighty but that I must earn my way into his good graces — which is impossible for me.

If God's promises are not true and his claims about himself are not true then we have nothing to stand on. We must believe that God is good, that he is powerful, that he truly loves us, that his promises are always true, and that he is willing to involve himself in every part of our lives. If we fail to believe these basic truths in any way, we will fail to trust God. If we don't trust him, we won't walk with him. We will begin to look for our security and significance in other places and in other relationships. We will chase the things of the world that promise those things. Career, power, money, relationships, and pleasure will move ahead of God on our list of pursuits. Fear will replace faith and we will have no anchor when the storms of life blow.

If I believe that God is good and powerful and loves, yet believe that I must constantly earn his love and approval to receive his blessings, then I am also in a hopeless position. We all fall short of the glory of God. That is why Jesus died for me. But if I forget or modify that truth, Satan will amplify my shortcomings, fill me with feelings of rejection, and convince me that I am outside the circle of God's care. Then I will begin to search elsewhere for my security and significance, believing that I am unworthy to receive these essential needs from such a great God.

Either strategy from the enemy will push me away from my heavenly Father. Satan expends a great deal of energy sowing lies in both of these areas that produce beliefs in opposition to the Word of God. His lies are effective.

Since the fall of man, our flesh rushes to agree with Satan. Our spiritual man must put on the armor of God and learn to wield divine weapons that push back the enemy lines in the world around us, and even in our own hearts.

Divine Weapons

God's goal for our lives is total transformation from the moment that we become a new creation in Christ to the moment that we are fully conformed to the image of his Son. Satan first wars to keep us from the salvation offered in Jesus Christ. Having failed in that attempt, he will work to keep us from being effective as believers and from claiming our destiny in Christ.

Although Satan may have established strongholds within us through lies, hurtful experiences, and sin, God has provided a number of "divine weapons" that, through the power of Christ, can tear down the strongholds that have hindered our joy, our peace and our service to God. Because Christ has fully paid the cost of our redemption on the cross, Satan has no legal claim on us and has no power over us except the power and authority we give him. The divine weapons Jesus provides do two things: they bring us into alignment or agreement with God (which nullifies Satan's authority to oppress us) and then they equip us to break the power of the enemy and destroy his works as representatives of Christ on this earth. Next we will discuss a few of those weapons.

The Holy Spirit — Power and Companionship

The Spirit sent by Jesus is a great force for healing and freedom that operates on our behalf. Jesus called him the "paraklete" (Jn. 14:16). He is "the one called to our side" which can be a helper, an advocate, a comforter, a counselor, or a faithful friend. He promised that his Spirit would be our teacher and source of truth (Jn. 14:17-26), revelation and wisdom (Eph. 1:7), direction (Rom. 8:14), intercession (Rom. 8:26), and power (Acts 1:8) to overcome the enemy.

Lies produce bondage. Truth sets us free. Wisdom and understanding keep us from stepping into Satan's traps. The fruit of the Spirit produced in our lives breaks the strength of the flesh and the power of the Holy Spirit equips us for battle. He is the presence of Jesus within us: healer, provider, deliverer — King of Kings and Lord of Lords.

Now the Lord is the Spirit, and where the Spirit of the Lord is, there is freedom. (2 Cor. 3:17)

The Word of God

In Paul's letter to the Ephesians, he counsels them to put on the armor of God to take their stand against the enemy. In his inventory of our armor, he declares that we are to take up the sword of the Spirit, which is the Word of God. Jesus overcame Satan in the wilderness by standing on the written Word of God three times. God's Word is truth. It pushes back and disarms the enemy. The promises of God are the firm ground on which we stand when assaulted by demons. God's Word, spoken and written, produces faith and the shield of faith and quenches the darts of the enemy. His Word lights our way. It is the plumb line by which we judge every action and every "revelation." It is living and active and keeps our heart turned toward God. "I have hidden your word in my heart that I might not sin against you." (Ps. 119:11) Knowing the Word and responding to the Word is essential to freedom in Christ. There is no substitute for time with God so that we might hear and receive his Word. The Word of God shaped the universe. It can also shape our hearts.

A Renewed Mind

Paul confirms this truth when he declares, "Do not conform any longer to the pattern of this world but be transformed by the renewing of your mind" (1 Cor. 12:2). Unlike the butterfly, our metamorphosis is not simply programmed in but is directly proportional to our willingness to submit to God with our mind, which includes our beliefs, attitudes, perspectives and decisions. It is coming to the place in our walk with God where our intellect and will give way to the thoughts, decisions, and priorities of his Spirit.

To have a renewed mind is to have the mind of Christ. Paul declares that we already possess the mind of Christ (1 Cor. 2:16). Like many things in the kingdom, we may possess something or have access to a spiritual blessing that we have not yet accessed or exercised. I possess a stationary bike but at this time in my life I make little use of it. The mind of Christ is in full agreement with the Father. The Spirit makes the mind of Christ available to us, but to make it ours, we must seek after his thoughts and perspectives, and pursue the Spirit of wisdom and revelation through prayer (and even fasting), and then condition our thoughts through obedience. As we partake of the mind of Christ, our own mind comes into agreement with the Father and the resources of the kingdom of heaven open up to us.

Obedience

It may seem strange to think of obedience as a divine weapon but it is the arena in which God sharpens our skills and gives us greater understanding of his ways. It is not enough to "know" the Word. We must be "doers" of the Word as well. Many principles of the Kingdom of God must be experienced before they can be understood. The apostles could not begin to experience the economic principles of heaven before they saw Jesus feed thousands out of one small lunch box. Without experiencing it, we have no reference point for understanding.

Most of the time, we must take action in faith and partnership with God before we find freedom from spiritual bondage. Many of Christ's commands call us to action before a spiritual blessing can be deposited in our account. Jesus sent ten lepers on their way to see the priest who would confirm their healing. They were healed as they went — not before they went. Jesus blessed Peter and his crew with so many fish that they thought their boats would sink, but they first had to lower their nets before experiencing God's provision. When it comes to freedom, as well as receiving other blessings in the kingdom, believing and doing are prerequisites.

When it comes to finding freedom and transformation in the Lord, this principle of obedience and action cannot be overstated. Too many of us view God as our fairy godmother who will appear one night to wave his magic wand over us and change everything, without any effort on our part. God rarely works that way. Palestine was promised. Victory was assured. Still, the Hebrews had to cross a river and fight many battles to experience the promise. James tells us that if anyone is sick, he should call the elders of the church to pray for him and to anoint him with oil. He goes on to say that we are to confess our sins one to another and pray for one another that we might be healed. The promise of healing calls for action on our part before the blessing will be experienced.

Another critical blessing that is related to obedience is revelation. Jesus said: "Whoever has my commands and obeys them, he is the one who loves me. He who loves me will be loved by my Father, and I too will love him and show myself to him." (John 14:21) Jesus promises that when we have been obedient to his teachings, he will give us more of himself. The more of Jesus we experience, the greater our healing, our freedom and our anointing will be.

Discipline

Another divine weapon or tool for profound life change is discipline. God is a Father. Loving fathers discipline their children. Sometimes, when we have walked outside the will of God, he allows us to experience hard things, brokenness, exposure, etc. so that we might come back under his authority and blessings. We should not hate nor resist his discipline but receive it, knowing that it will lead to greater transformation on our part.

"My son, do not make light of the Lord's discipline, and do not lose heart when he rebukes you, because the Lord disciplines those he loves, and he punishes everyone he accepts as a son. Endure hardship as discipline; God is treating you as sons. For what son is not disciplined by his father? No discipline seems pleasant at the time, but painful. Later on, however, it produces a harvest of righteousness and peace for those who have been trained by it." (Heb. 12:5-11)

Confession

Confession is a powerful tool for transformation. Confession simply means to say what God has said about something (anything). When we confess Christ, we are saying what God has said about him. We are coming into agreement with God and aligning our thoughts with his truth. When we confess sin in our lives, we are saying what God has said about that thing and are coming into agreement with him about our sinful thoughts or behaviors.

The discipline of confession keeps us aligned with God so that we don't fall into agreement with Satan. To do so gives him authority to oppress us in that area of our life. That is why James counsels us, "Is any one of you sick? He should call the elders of the church to pray over him and anoint him with oil in the name of the Lord. And the prayer offered in faith will make the sick person well; the Lord will raise him up. If he has sinned, he will be forgiven. Therefore, confess your sins to each other and pray for each other that you may be healed." (James 5:14-16)

Confession in this context opens us up for healing whether in the physical, emotional or spiritual realm. Notice that some conditions of illness are related to sin that needs to be forgiven. It is not that God has visited this sin on his people but that their sin has given Satan access to them. Confession then reveals the sin, nullifies Satan's right to oppress them, and brings the sinner into alignment with God again so that his healing grace can flow to them.

In the case of emotional wounds that need to be healed, opening up to others allows God to clean out the bitterness, shame and fear as others minister love, grace and acceptance to that person. Confession is a form of transparency that allows light to shine into dark places for cleansing and healing. For most of us, healing is greatly needed before real transformation can occur in our lives. Healing comes through openness with God and with others. Confession opens the door to healing.

Confession and transparency is acknowledging our sin and weakness and taking personal responsibility for our choices. Then, by faith, we are to lay our sin at the foot of the cross and press in to God for healing and freedom from the wounds that have been catalysts for our sinful or self-destructive behaviors. Our first step to healing and freedom from any form of bondage is to "own" our sin and our brokenness. Until I own something I can't give it away. Until I own my sin and my bondage, I can't give it to Jesus. When we blame others or excuse our own sinful or hurtful actions towards others, we limit the work of God within us and give Satan access to us through our own denial.

On the other hand, "If we confess our sins, he is faithful and just to forgive us our sins and to cleanse us from all unrighteousness" (1 John 1:9). The word *cleanse* in this verse means to *purify* or *to remove a stain*. I believe that as we own our actions and attitudes and agree with God, that his standards are right and just. When we confess them with a heart of repentance, God not only forgives the sin but he also begins to take the stain of that sin out of the fabric of our lives. He begins to heal us of our shame, our overpowering sense of worthlessness, and our nagging fear that ultimately we, nor our needs, matter to anyone. When those stains are removed, then we are healed and our transformation will move ahead.

Self-Examination

Obviously, self-examination is a key to confession. We can't confess those things we are unaware of. But most of us become aware of our issues only as they become disruptive forces in our lives. Many issues could be resolved as wounds or temptations before they manifest as sin and destructive behaviors in our lives and relationships if they were recognized, talked about, prayed about, and submitted to the blood of Christ. Sin tends to take on a life of its own if it is not dealt when it is just beginning to sprout. Pulling up weeds when they are small and haven't developed an extensive root system is much easier than waiting until the weed and its offspring are taking over the garden.

My wife Susan and I have a back yard that we have labored in. We certainly have a "post curse" yard that, like Eden after the curse, does not cooperate with our efforts. When we bought our house, we noticed the lovely trumpet vines beginning to grow along the fence in our back yard. Unlike everything else in our West Texas flowerbed, this vine flourished. It grew green. It grew tall. It grew at lightning speed. Quickly, it attached itself to our cedar picket fence. Initially, it was gorgeous, displaying deep green leaves with bright orange flowers.

Like sin, though it was pleasant in the beginning, by the end of summer it was growing between the cedar pickets of our fence and pushing them away from the stringers they were attached to. The sheer weight of the vine would soon be more than mere cedar could withstand. But worse, its runners were going everywhere, choking out the other plants in the bed. So, with vengeance in our hearts, we decided to destroy the monster that was devouring our yard. We had not stopped it when it was young but we determined to take it out now. But then we discovered how evil the vine truly was. Underground, in the darkness where no one could see, it had sent out root systems all over the yard. If you cut it and poisoned it here, it simply sprang up there. To try to pull it up was almost impossible. To take out the root system we would have to destroy the entire flowerbed and parts of the yard. So now, like strategies against terrorists, we have moved from the idea of eradication to merely containment.

Sin is like that trumpet vine. If left unchecked it digs in deep. It sends out runners. It may begin with checking out a few porn sites just out of curiosity. But then it keeps calling you back and soon becomes a semi-regular habit, then a regular habit, then an overpowering need. Shame becomes part of your life. Secrecy slips in and begins to foster distrust in your marriage. On and on it goes. Sin has sent out its runners and its root systems have gone deep into your life. Unlike our failing battle to control trumpet vine, Christ does have the power to uproot the deepest sin in our lives. How much easier would it have been had you simply examined yourself in the beginning and dealt with sin when it was a seedling in your life, rather than digging it up when it is full grown with an extensive root system?

Regular self-examination is a good thing. Take a regular inventory of your thoughts, your actions, and the things that you know are "borderline" thoughts and behaviors. Dealing with them quickly through confession, prayer and transparency will save your spiritual fences and flowerbeds from a great deal of pain.

But if we judged ourselves, we would not come under judgment"
(1 Cor. 11:31)

Search me, O God, and know my heart; test me and know my anxious
thoughts. See if there is any offensive way in me, and lead me in the
way everlasting. (Ps. 139:23-24)

Persistent Prayer

Prayer is the most powerful weapon in the believer's arsenal, as prayer nurtures
our personal relationship with the Father and moves God to act on our behalf.
James tells believers that we often *"have not because we ask not"* (James 4:2).
The implication of this and many other scriptures is that there are numerous
things God is willing to do and even desires to do, but will not do until we
ask. Our asking, however, prompts the exercise of God's unlimited power on
our behalf (when our requests are aligned with his purposes). Our prayers
can move God to protect, heal, deliver, provide, change our hearts, soften the
hearts of others, and even launch war in the heavenly realms as he acts for us.

In the book of Daniel, we are given an interesting revelation of things that
occur in the spiritual realm in response to a believer's prayer. It also emphasizes
the overriding need to continue in prayer. The prophet had received a disturbing
dream. Rather than making assumptions about the meaning of the dream,
Daniel began to pray and fast, asking God to give him the understanding of
the things he had been shown. For twenty-one days, Daniel continued to seek
the Lord and the interpretation. On the twenty-first day of Daniel's fast, the
prophet was visited by an angel in a vision. The angel had come to give him
understanding of his dream. What the angel shares with Daniel is instructive.

Since the first day that you set your mind to gain understanding and
to humble yourself before your God, your words were heard, and I
have come in response to them. But the prince of the Persian kingdom
resisted me twenty-one days. Then Michael, one of the chief princes,
came to help me, because I was detained there with the king of Persia.
Now I have come to explain to you what will happen to your people
in the future. (Dan. 10:12-14)

It is not only imperative that we pray, but that we keep on praying.
Prayer sets things in motion in the spiritual realm, but the enemy also moves

to resist the response of God. Many of our prayers are answered through angelic activity. "Are not all angels ministering spirits sent to serve those who will inherit salvation?" (Heb. 1:14) And many of our prayers are resisted by demonic activity. As Daniel prayed, a heavenly battle was taking place on his behalf. His part was to pray and (this is important) to keep praying until he heard from God. If Daniel had not continued to pray and fast for an answer would Michael have been dispatched to take up the battle? Would the angel have continued his mission to find Daniel or would he have been turned back?

Prayer is a divine weapon that sets the heavenly realms in motion. Much more is going on related to our prayers than we can see. How often have we prayed half-heartedly for something? How often have we prayed but quickly became discouraged because we didn't see our prayer being answered? How often have we quit praying about an issue long before we should have? We should never under estimate the power of prayer. It moves God, his angels, and the Holy Spirit to act on our behalf when it is consistent with the heart and ways of God, when it is fervent, and when it is persistent. "The prayer of a righteous man is powerful and effective" (James 5:16). Keep praying for the freedom and transformation in your life that Jesus has purchased for you.

Spiritual Authority

At times, believers need to directly confront the enemy with the authority of Jesus Christ. When the enemy comes against us with temptation, discouragement, or accusation we have authority as citizens of heaven who represent Christ on this earth to deal with the assault. If we were not subject to assault, Paul would not have instructed us to put on the armor of God (Eph. 6:11). Those assaults or "schemes" are not a matter of "if" but "when." We will be attacked and when we are, Paul instructs us to stand rather than run. We stand in the authority and power of Jesus Christ.

In the gospels, we see Jesus move in power and authority over disease, demons, and even the elements. The gospels tell us that Jesus also transferred his power and authority to his followers so that they too might confirm the kingdom by preaching the gospel, healing the sick, and casting out demons. He gave that power first to his twelve apostles, then to seventy-two other miscellaneous believers that he sent out on brief mission trips to Israel. Both groups reported on their return that even demons were subject to them in the name of Jesus. But Jesus didn't stop there.

Jesus said, "I tell you the truth, anyone who has faith in me will do what I have been doing. He will do even greater things than these because I am going to the Father. And I will do whatever you ask in my name, so that the Son may bring glory to the Father" (John 14:12). His parting command, recorded in the gospel of Matthew, was that his followers should go into all the world, preach the gospel and make disciples. This command is often called "the great commission." In this case, it would certainly be a co-mission with Jesus, joining his followers to continue what he began on the earth.

He began this commission by declaring that he had been given all authority in heaven and on earth and finished it with a promise that he would be with his followers (co-mission) until the end of the age. His consistent model for fulfilling that command while he was on the earth was to preach the gospel and to demonstrate the kingdom by exercising his authority for healing and deliverance. After his ascension, he sent the Holy Spirit to empower his church for the same mission. As followers of Jesus, we also are to use his power and authority to overcome the enemy in our own lives and the lives of others.

Jesus still has all authority in heaven and on earth. He is still working through his people. Those he commissions he empowers. Those he appoints he anoints. Believers can still confront the powers of darkness with heaven's power and authority and must do so on many occasions. We will discuss the spiritual authority of believers in greater detail later in this book.

Personal Reflection / Journaling:

- God is in the business of change. How has he changed you since you came to Jesus Christ?
- What "tools" has he already used to make those changes?
- Ask him to show you the transformation that has already taken place in you, even if it is not clear to you.
- Over the next few days, reflect on the changes in your life since you became a believer. Have you changed dramatically or have you barely changed since coming to Christ? Have you been liberated in some areas of your life but know that strongholds still exist in other parts? Which divine weapons have you employed consistently as you have invited God to change you? What areas of your life have you not yet surrendered to Christ for change?

Memory Verse:

"The weapons we fight with are not the weapons of the world. On the contrary, they have divine power to demolish strongholds. We demolish arguments and every pretension that sets itself up against the knowledge of God, and we take captive every thought to make it obedient to Christ."

(2 Cor. 10:4)

Prayer Focus: Ask God to show you areas in your life including beliefs, attitudes, and behaviors that he wants to change. Write down the areas he shows you and begin earnestly to invite him to make those changes in you.

Suggested Prayer:

Father in heaven, in the name of Jesus, I ask you to search me and show me any offensive ways within me. I pray as your servant David prayed, "Search my heart O God and show me any offensive ways." Father I want to be like Jesus in every way. In his name, I now renounce the flesh and all the works of Satan that have been present in my life. I surrender my heart, my mind, and my actions to the Lordship of Jesus Christ. Now I ask you Holy Spirit to change me from the inside out as you see fit, in Jesus' name...Amen.

Chapter Seven

LEVELS OF CHANGE

And we, who with unveiled faces all reflect the Lord's glory, are being transformed into his likeness with ever-increasing glory, which comes from the Lord, who is the Spirit. (2 Cor. 3:18)

Transformation is in the human heart. Deep inside, we know we are not yet what we ought to be. We sense the defectiveness that resides within our fallen nature. As a result, we are restless. We seek something to change us or our lives believing that when we have been changed, we will be the person we long to be — significant, confident, loved, and at peace. Most of the world is looking in all the wrong places for the magic formula that will transfigure them from who they are to the person they believe they want to be. When they find their "silver bullet" for transformation, it falls short. Then they are off on another quest. The problem is that not all change is the same. The alchemy peddled by Madison Avenue is superficial and fleeting and falls short of godly change that is profound and eternal. This chapter will examine three levels of change, clarify why most attempts at transformation fall short, and then point you to the profound change that God offers you.

How can a man be born when he is old?" Nicodemus asked. "Surely he cannot enter a second time into his mother's womb to be born!" Jesus answered, "I tell you the truth, no one can enter the Kingdom of God unless he is born of water and the Spirit...You must be born again. (John 3:4-7)

In the text above, Jesus and Nicodemus had a brief theological discussion about life change. Nicodemus held the position that, when it is all said and done, a man is who he is and that is all he will ever be. He may clean up a little with a few cosmetic changes, but his character is set and essentially, nothing ever truly changes in the inner man.

Jesus, however, declared that a man can be radically and essentially changed by an encounter with God. The phrase "born again" can also be translated "born from above." It implies that God is able to do something in us (even in our wretchedly fallen state) that changes everything. Paul said it this way, "If anyone is in Christ, he is a new creation; the old has gone, the new has come" (2 Cor. 5:17)!

World-View

Today we see a paradox in the world's view of transformation. On one hand, advertising offers an endless number of products that promise to change a person forever. On the other hand, secular science tells us that who we are is mostly determined by chemistry and genetics. If we are born to be alcoholic, then that is who we will be, drunk or sober, forever in recovery. If we are homosexual, it was genetically determined and nothing can change that. If we are violent, brain chemistry makes it inevitable and only science can hope to save us. If that is the case we cannot truly change.

The truth is that the world is right. Man cannot essentially change by his own efforts. Our fallen nature makes us slaves to sin (Rom. 6:20). We can provide techniques and drugs to help manage socially disruptive behaviors, or we can declare behaviors "good" that were once thought to be sinful, but we can't really change the person at his core. Jesus actually agreed with that position but offered another option...to *be born from above*. Jesus offered the possibility of a supernatural intervention beyond the scope of psychiatry or science that can change a man at his core.

Jesus pointed to an encounter with God and his Spirit that can alter the very makeup of a man. Think about it. Encounters with God changed physiology: the man born blind suddenly saw everything, the lame jumped to their feet, and the deaf heard sounds they never imagined.

Even greater miracles were performed on the hearts of men. Jews and gentiles, who had hated each other for centuries, became one in Christ. Women, who had been treated as property, were accepted as honored leaders in the church. Political terrorists disposed of their daggers. Unscrupulous tax collectors gave their wealth away. Homosexuals and prostitutes received healing for the wounds that drove them to their lifestyles. That was the good news of the Kingdom of God. It still is. It is the gospel of change, offered by a God who never changes.

Levels of Change

When we talk about change, it is helpful to consider the nature of change itself. Some "change" is strictly cosmetic. A little makeup, a coat of paint, a few new clothes, or a little therapeutic language can give the appearance of change — but a little observation reveals that essentially everything is the same. Then there are levels of change that impact our behaviors but not our values or perspectives. We may act in different ways but essentially our core beliefs and values stay the same. We trade in old strategies for new ones to get what we want, but what we want has not changed. Then there are levels of change that affect us to the core. These are the truly transformative levels that God offers his people through his Spirit and an encounter with Jesus Christ. Let's look at these three levels in more detail.

Three Levels of Change

Level One change is *environmental change*. This is the least powerful level. Often people believe that changing their surroundings will free them from their hurt, emptiness, or inability to maintain relationships. They move from job to job, house to house, and relationship to relationship, believing that whatever they are looking for will be found in the next location, the next friendship, or even the next marriage. Yet, in every situation, they have been the common denominator. Refusing to look within to see if their brokenness is the root cause of their problems, they continue to change environments, doing the same things, getting the same results and feeling victimized with each failure.

Level Two change is *behavioral or cognitive change*, which includes conscious thoughts, feelings, and actions. This is where most people, counselors, self-help programs, and even churches focus their attention. At this level, we examine our thoughts about a person, a situation, or even ourselves and try to replace those specific thoughts with more positive or even more biblical thoughts. We identify hurtful or sinful actions and replace those with more positive actions. We challenge our emotions and try to change those by changing our thoughts or our actions. We adopt positive thinking, loving behaviors, acting our way into feeling better, etc. This level of change can be effective in helping us manage destructive issues. However, in many cases it does not go to the root cause of the destructive behavior or debilitating emotions.

Individuals at this level often spend a great deal of time and energy "keeping the lid on" issues with new coping techniques they have learned through counseling, reading, or even from the pulpit. When they tire, when outside stresses take their toll, or when the other person in their life isn't coping with his or her own issues, then the "lid" usually comes off. This level of change is usually accomplished in our own strength and can be accomplished by believers as well as unbelievers without the help of God.

Level Three change is *heart change*. Scripture differentiates between the heart and mind, as we are told to love the Lord with all our heart and mind. The deepest level of change is found in our heart, or what the Bible calls our "inmost being" (Ps. 139:13). It is in our "heart" that **core beliefs** about God and about ourselves reside. It seems that "the heart" is the part of our being where thoughts, emotions, and beliefs are deep, powerful, and not always known by us, although they are manifested in our spontaneous words and actions. "But the things that come out of the mouth come from the heart, and these make a man 'unclean.' For out of the heart come evil thoughts, murder, adultery, sexual immorality, theft, false testimony, slander." (Matt. 15:18-19)

In our cultural model, our concept of the *subconscious* might be closest to the biblical concept of *the heart* although in the biblical concept we seem to have the capacity to know the deep thoughts of our heart, at least by revelation, and to guard that arena of our thinking and feeling (Prov. 4:23).

We can also think one thing with our mind and another thing with our heart. That may be the source of the internal debates we often have with ourselves or the biblical concept of "double-mindedness." When our 'mind thoughts" line up with our "heart thoughts", then we experience what therapists call "congruence" and a wholehearted approach to life can be possible. Most of us, however, are not there yet.

We have all had the experience of believing something at a cognitive, rational or intellectual level, while knowing that something deep inside did not agree with the beliefs we held in our mind. For instance, we might say…

- I know I am forgiven…but I don't feel forgiven.
- I know I have no apparent reason to be afraid… but I am full of anxiety.
- I know that God loves me… but I don't feel loved.
- Part of me thinks this, but another part of me thinks…

The Power of Core Beliefs

Beliefs in our hearts have the power to shape and affect everything else we do. These beliefs are most often created by experiences in our past, usually in childhood. As children, we try to make sense of our experiences and come to conclusions about life, God, or ourselves based on the limited understanding and perspectives of childhood. These core beliefs are rarely taught to us in any formal way. Instead, experiences and our conclusions drawn from these experiences create these basic beliefs through which the rest of life is filtered. Typically these powerful beliefs are experienced more as feelings than articulated thoughts. They may be positive or negative in content.

These *core beliefs* may reflect one or more of the perspectives listed below:

- God exists / There is no God
- God is good / God is bad
- God loves me / God hates me / God is indifferent toward me
- God is all powerful / God is not all powerful
- God can be trusted / God cannot be trusted
- God keeps his promises / God only keeps his promises sometimes
- God is involved in my life / God only watches
- God looks out for me / I am on my own / God is out to get me
- God is a loving Father / God is a scorekeeper waiting to punish
- I am significant / I don't matter
- I am lovable / I am unworthy of love
- I am capable / I am inadequate
- I am acceptable / I am defective
- Etc.

These core beliefs shape how we face life, receive or give love, manage setbacks, face challenges, pray, worship, trust, forgive or fail to forgive, and just about every other decision we will make.

Through the years I have worked with several female survivors of Satanic Ritual Abuse. As children these women were abused by satanic cults. Some developed multiple personalities as a way to cope with what they had experienced; others did not. But all were deeply affected by their experiences as a child. The deep seated beliefs they carried with them as a result of those experiences shaped their lives in profound ways.

Imagine being six years old, taken through mysterious ceremonies by strangers dressed in robes, surrounded by candles, chanting things you could not understand. Imagine being sexually violated and witnessing animal sacrifices. Imagine being prayed over in the name of Satan or taken through a ceremony in which you were betrothed to Lucifer. Imagine this happening on several occasions. Imagine that all of this was cloaked in secrecy and fear. No one discussed the event with you. If you tried to talk about it you were dismissed or told it was just a dream. If you had to make sense of it as a six-year-old girl, what beliefs might be formed in you as a result of your experience? I can tell you what most of the children believed who went through this kind of experience and they carried these beliefs into their adulthood.

Most believed that there was something terribly wrong and terribly unacceptable about them. Otherwise, why would their parents or God allow something like that to be done to them? Most of them carried a deep sense of shame about what they had "participated in." They saw the world as a frightening place where they could be helplessly victimized again at any moment. Their view of God was that he didn't care about them because he didn't rescue them from the cult. If he did care, he couldn't rescue them so Satan must be more powerful than God. They had no reason to trust anyone in authority, especially religious figures, and believed that they must control their lives and relationships at every level or something just as terrifying might happen again.

In their teen and adult years these beliefs manifested in coping mechanisms of drug abuse, drinking, depression, promiscuity, anger, manipulation, distrust, and profound feelings of being violated by almost any person who failed to affirm them or meet a need. Obviously, long-term relationships and even happiness was a challenge for each of these women. Rational discussion of the causes of their behaviors would not heal these wounds any more than being aware that cigarettes cause lung cancer will heal that disease. These women understood that their responses to the events around them were irrational but had no ability to respond in other ways. Most depended on antidepressants or other "drugs of choice" to get through the day as they continued to feel unloved and unlovable.

We could all step back from their experiences and tell them that their perceptions were untrue — that they were amazing survivors of something terrible and that God did love them. We could tell them that there were people in the world they could trust and that even their spouses had their best interests at heart. We could tell them that God would walk with them through hard times if they trusted in him. We "know" that all these things are true. But, in nearly every case, conclusions drawn from experiences trump our intellectual beliefs every time. The heart rules the head not just in matters of love but in beliefs and perspectives as well.

Most of us were not handed over to satanic cults as children. But, as children, we have experienced our own rejection, abuse, abandonment, loss, shame, indifference, and betrayal. Depending upon the severity or the frequency of these experiences we possess our own core beliefs about life, God, and ourselves. These are lenses though which we filter our current experiences and shape our response to the people or situations presently in our lives. Positive childhood experiences may create self-confidence, trust in God, and an expectation of positive outcomes in life. Negative experiences create just the opposite.

I have spent most of my ministry with the wounded, doubting, fearful sheep in God's flock. But I know others full of joy, confidence, and optimism because they had positive, life—giving experiences as children. And also I know others (here is the good news) who walk that way now because they have been healed by God — including those traumatized by Satanists. *Level Three* change touches us in these deepest areas of our beliefs and when those are changed, we are changed radically. I believe that only God can truly touch these places and bring healing through Christ's touch and his truth.

We all have a fallen nature. As a result, genetics and brain chemistry are distorted. Hurting people hurt other people and we carry the wounds of those encounters. But the greater truth is Jesus Christ who has come to heal hearts that have been broken and bodies that have been twisted. If an encounter with Christ can restore sight, cleanse lepers, and grow limbs then it can also heal our broken genetics and physiology if those, indeed, push us uncontrollably toward sin. The truth that sets us free can uproot lies about who we are and who God is and set us free from the prisons and captivity of our past. Jesus is the God who heals. The next few chapters will discuss practical ways to access the healing promised by God and purchased by Christ.

Personal Reflection / Journaling:

- What levels of change have you experienced in your life?
- What is left that needs healing by the touch of God?
- Continue to Ask God to show you places in your heart that he still wants to touch with his healing power. Trust him to be gentle.

Memory Verse:
"I pray also that the eyes of your heart may be enlightened in order that you may know the hope to which he has called you, the riches of his glorious inheritance in the saints, and his incomparably great power for us who believe." (Eph. 1:18-19)

Suggested Prayer:
Father, you are the God of transformation. Lord, I ask you to touch every place in me that hinders my ability to love you and to love others, Father, I give you full permission to show me the places we need to visit together so that I might be fully free. Lord, give me greater faith and greater trust for the journey. In Jesus' name... Amen.

Chapter Eight

HEALING YOUR SOUL

He leads me beside quiet waters, he restores my soul. (Psm. 23:2-3)

The Healing Power of the Truth

Nearly every believer can quote the words of Jesus, "You will know the truth and the truth will set you free" (John 8:32). Jesus followed that statement by also declaring that he is the truth (see John 14:6), the full revelation of God's will and the reality of God's kingdom on earth. Both what Jesus said and did reveal the true heart of the Father. His heart is to heal and set free.

This chapter will give you a deeper understanding of the process of healing and show you how to access the healing that Jesus has already purchased for you through his suffering. "He himself bore our sins in his body on the tree, so that we might die to sins and live for righteousness; by his wounds you have been healed." (1 Pet. 2:24)

It is important to know the heart of God. There is a stream of Christian thinking that promotes the idea that sometimes God is the source of suffering and brokenness in our lives since these kinds of things can draw us closer to him or open doors for Christian ministry to others wounded as we have been. To say that God can use suffering and tragedies for kingdom purposes is not the same as saying that he is their source or that he approved of the suffering.

Jesus said that if we have seen him we have seen the Father (John 14:9). Whatever Jesus hated, God hates and whatever Jesus loved, God loves. Jesus said and demonstrated that he came to forgive, heal, and set broken people free in body, soul and spirit. Nowhere in the gospels do we ever see Jesus impart disease, suffering, or tragedy to others as sources of spiritual blessing and purification. We do see him deliver men and women from those conditions time after time.

We never see Jesus extending grace to some while heaping shame on others who came to him for healing as if a little more shame, rejection, and condemnation would do them good. What we do see is the compassionate heart of God who is willing to heal and set free, regardless of the sin that drew people into prisons of their own making. As we seek healing from God, we can be assured that he is willing.

Alignment

Healing is ultimately based on coming into alignment with God's truth. Adam and Eve led us into a labyrinth of sin and brokenness when they believed and acted on Satan's lies. God's truth is the map that takes us out of the labyrinth. When a body is healed it is because it has realigned itself with God's will for the human body; this is his blueprint and purpose for each part. Our spirit is revived and we are born again because we have aligned ourselves with God through faith and repentance. When we are emotionally broken and in bondage to enemy strongholds, healing and freedom come only when we align ourselves with God's truth about us and his unwavering love for us — as seen in Christ and the cross.

We have many core beliefs established through hurtful experiences that do not line up with the truth of God's Word. We mistakenly came to believe these "lies" when we had no framework of truth through which to filter our experiences. What we truly believe about ourselves, God, and life colors every thought we have, every feeling we experience, and every decision we make. The enemy establishes these beliefs in us, or reinforces existing beliefs, through his use of other people or through demonic thoughts whispered in our minds.

An abused or neglected child will often take on the belief that she is being abused or neglected because there is something about her that is bad, unworthy of love, or deserving of rejection and abuse. Insecurity, hypersensitivity and fear of abandonment will paint that child's relationships in adulthood.

The constantly criticized child will take on the belief that love is based on performance and is only granted when an individual performs "perfectly" the demands of others...including God. That child may become the "overachiever" or perfectionist desperately trying to fill the void of affirmation in his life by the praise he receives from others when he succeeds. Alternately, that child may be become the discouraged child who believes that no matter what, his efforts will never be good enough. Fear of failure and rejection will produce a "driven" adult, one who never risks failure, or one who rationalizes every shortcoming in his life by blaming others.

Children who have lost loved ones through death or abandonment may believe that whomever they love will inevitably be taken away or leave them. To protect themselves from the inevitable pain of loss, they may live a life where emotional attachments and intimacy are minimal, if they exist at all.

Such "misbeliefs" (or "lies") go beyond a conviction that we have done something wrong. More than that, they convince us that there is something wrong with us that will eventually keep others, including God, from loving us and will surely keep us from succeeding or receiving the blessings other people enjoy.

We may also act in ways that reinforce these beliefs. For instance, a person who thinks she will eventually be rejected by people may remain at a distance, be defensive and hypersensitive to criticism, or may even use anger as a defense mechanism. Those behaviors will eventually drive others away and then confirm the wounded individual's beliefs that sooner or later people will reject her. The child who believes that he is incapable may carry so much pressure to succeed that the pressure keeps him from performing well...thus confirming the view he holds about himself.

An abused child, a molested child, a child whose parents died, etc. may not only take on negative beliefs about herself, she may also believe that God is indifferent to her pain, is powerless to help, or is sadistic — taking things from her that she needs most. Satan whispers those thoughts in the mind of a child whenever possible to establish lies that shape every decision in that person's life from that point on. Unless those core beliefs are changed, as much as truth sets us free, lies keep us in bondage.

Paul tells us that the mind (the thought life) is the real battleground for the believer (2 Cor. 10:3-5). Our goal then, is to take every thought (conscious and subconscious) and align it with the truth of Jesus Christ. God uses many tools at all three levels of change to reconstruct us but the greatest transformation occurs as we align our core beliefs and intellect with God's truth. "Do not conform any longer to the pattern of this world, but be transformed by the renewing of your mind." (Rom. 12:2) When our mind is aligned with our heart and our heart is aligned with God's Spirit, then we are renewed.

God's truth can find its way to our heart in many ways, but the most powerful way is through revelation, where God's Spirit bears witness with our spirit about his truth so that the life-giving Word of God replaces a lie that has affected us for years (Rom. 8:16). The lies of Satan are deadly but the truth of Jesus Christ gives life. Adam bit on Satan's lie in the Garden and death entered into the world. But when Jesus touched the dead, the dead breathed again. When Jesus touches a lie, he drains it of its deadly poison and breathes his healing truth into a wound that was releasing its toxin into our life.

Indicators

The following is a list of indicators that suggest that unhealed wounds and strongholds exist in an individual's life. You may want to highlight any that you recognize in your own life or in the life of someone you love so that you can seek healing from Jesus in each area of brokenness.

- *A preoccupation with certain hurtful events from the past.* When we keep remembering traumatic events from our past, perhaps even making decisions based on them or the people involved in the event, then healing is needed. Until we are healed and the wounding lies are replaced with God's truth, we will continue to be tied to our past and unable to move ahead, especially in relationships.

- *Overreaction and deep pain stirred by things someone says or does in the present.* When we have a pattern of overreacting to the common weaknesses of people and the things they say, we are experiencing the pain not just from that moment but from all our past moments connected to our current experience. That moment is like someone accidently bumping into an old shoulder wound that has never properly healed. If that person had brushed your other shoulder, you would hardly have noticed but when they bump into your existing wound, you suddenly feel all the pain stored up in that wound. Unfortunately, we tend to blame the one who bumped into us for all the pain we experience in that moment, even though the real pain came from a past wound they did not inflict. We react the same way when someone brushes an emotional wound we carry.

- *An inability to truly receive love or connect emotionally with others.* When we are wounded, our greatest need is to be loved. Our greatest fear is that once someone discovers who we really are, they will reject us. Some individuals fear rejection to such an extent that they cannot risk intimacy because intimacy makes them known. They carry a deep-seated belief that they are unworthy of love and that they cannot receive it nor trust it when it is given. For these individuals, relationships are just too risky. They avoid deep connections assuming that sooner or later they will be rejected.

- *An inability to forgive those who have "hurt" you or "wronged" you.* For deeply wounded people, unforgiveness is functional. Our refusal to forgive keeps negative emotions alive that we believe protect us from further hurt. Our anger and resentment keep the offending parties at bay so that they cannot get close enough to ever hurt us again. Unforgiveness fosters distrust, which keeps every person at a distance so that we will never again be injured by anyone. Having been "victimized" in the past, we despise feelings of weakness or vulnerability, so we choose anger and aggression to cloak our fear. Our unforgiveness also allows us to blame those who wronged us for all of our problems so that we never have to take responsibility for our contributions or own our weaknesses.

I have also known individuals who refused to forgive, believing that if they forgave their tormentors then God would forgive their tormentors and justice would be thwarted. Brenda was a committed Christian woman whose second marriage was on the verge of collapse. On a daily basis, Brenda would fly into a rage and "slice and dice" her husband with a razor sharp tongue for seemingly innocent things he did or said. He loved her deeply but was at the end of his matrimonial rope.

Her past was poisoning her present. Years earlier she had married, had two daughters with her young husband, and then watched as he was drafted and deployed to Vietnam. After two years, he returned home but the war had changed him. He was frighteningly abusive towards Brenda. He beat her, choked her, and on occasion held a pistol to her head and promised to kill her. She lived in constant fear for her life. One day, in a state of terror, she left for the grocery store and just kept driving, leaving her two daughters with him.

Plagued with guilt about abandoning her girls and filled with hatred toward her first husband, Brenda was taking her pain out on her second husband. Although she had soon reconnected with her daughters to assure their safety the toxicity from her anger and bitterness towards her "ex" was poisoning her current marriage. One day, I asked Brenda, "So...when are you going to forgive your first husband?" With fists clenched, teeth clamped and veins popping on her neck, this proper young woman hissed, "Forgive him! I hope he burns in hell for what he has done to me!" Brenda knew the biblical teaching on forgiveness but could not bring herself to release her anger toward the "ex." It helped to mask her own feelings of guilt and weakness for leaving her girls with him.

As we talked, it became clear that she believed her forgiveness would compel God to forgive him. Justice would never be done. Eventually, Brenda understood that forgiveness was a healing balm for the wounded rather than a free pass for the offender. Forgiving her "ex" released Brenda from her past and the poison in her soul. Brenda was able to turn judgment of her former spouse over to God and even pray for him to come to Christ. After forgiving, her second marriage was healed and began to flourish.

- *An inability to take responsibility for wrongs done to others or personal failures while you consistently excuse yourself and blame others.* This dynamic is again attached to our fear that we are ultimately unworthy of love and a belief that love must be constantly earned by perfection or high levels of performance. Somehow, these individuals have come to believe that personal weakness or imperfections will cause others to reject them. Therefore, they cover their imperfections at all costs and deflect all responsibility for any failure to others. These individuals inadvertently drive others away by their blaming and insistence on being right.
- *The persistent feeling that you are a victim.* This manifestation of unhealed wounds and strongholds is a persistent, demanding feeling that you are being personally wronged or betrayed when things don't go your way. Because you have been victimized in the past, you may feel entitled to preferential treatment in the present. You feel wronged

or even betrayed when someone says "no," or doesn't live up to your expectations. You feel helpless to change the things in your life and believe that others should change them for you. Anger and bitterness are usually deeply engrained strongholds in this unhealed person.

- *Addictions.* All types of addictions are manifestations of strongholds or negative belief systems. Addictions are usually an individual's way of medicating his pain and feeling significant or powerful for a moment. Drugs, alcohol, sexual addictions, gambling, buying, eating — all these can indicate a great deal of unhealed brokenness in a person's life.

- *General Indicators.* In general, any area of your life that is out of control, that you obsess about or medicate, or about you are persistently driven by strong emotions, indicate a need for inner healing. A history of broken relationships, trauma as a child (abuse, neglect, sexual wounding), or any fearful event or significant loss that was never talked about or normalized, also suggests the need for God's touch in those deep places.

Each of these areas can point to a stronghold that has developed in your life, which hinders your joy, your love, and your effectiveness as a believer. A personal experience with God or Jesus is the most profound source of healing for these strongholds. Jesus came to set captives free and a word from him is the ultimate healing experience that we all need and should pursue.

Finding Healing in the Lord

When I was a child growing up in Amarillo, Texas, my grandmother lived in an old two-story house. The upstairs was one large room with a sitting area at one end and a small bedroom arrangement at the other. In that room was a closet and at the back of the closet was a smaller door cut to provide access to the attic. When it was opened it seemed dark and eerie to me.

I don't remember who, but someone told me that the "bogeyman" lived on the other side of that door and if I misbehaved, he would creep out in the dark of night and do unspeakable things to me. When I spent the night at my grandmother's house, I had to sleep upstairs in that room. The last thing I would have ever done was to open that door. The truth was that no "bogeyman" lived behind the door. My fears of destruction were unfounded. But to discover that truth and believe it in my heart, the door would have to be opened and the attic exposed with light, showing me that there was really nothing to fear.

When we, as believers, continue to live with guilt, shame and fear from our past it is because we have not fully opened those secret places to Jesus. We may fear his rejection or that the pain of remembering will be beyond our ability to endure once more. Deciding to go with him into those secret places so that he might shine the light of his truth and love on our past is critical to healing. It is not that he withholds healing but that we withhold access. So I invite you to finally trust Jesus for truth and healing in those areas of your life. If there are still secret places you have not visited with the Healer, identify those places and make a decision to visit the secret places with him soon.

God heals us in many ways but one of the most intentional approaches is simply to ask God to deal with individual hurts or memories that continue to create pain for us. This is where "trusting God" becomes essential to our healing. Sometimes, going back in our memories and reliving the initial experience helps us gain a new perspective, for it allows the Holy Spirit to apply the truth of Jesus Christ to the lie that was established when we first had that experience.

As we go back, we can experience that moment with God's truth, the presence of Jesus, and the maturity of adulthood to help us know the truth about that situation. Paul wrote, "When I was a child, I talked like a child, I thought like a child, I reasoned like a child. When I became a man, I put childish ways behind me." (1 Cor. 13:11) As Jesus speaks to us about the experience, his "revealed truth" is written on our heart and overwrites the old, false belief. God's Word, especially his spoken word, has power to create and to transform. It is amazing to see the transformation and healing of hearts as God speaks to his children in those places. In the same way that the words of Christ can heal bodies, they can also heal hearts. The memory stays intact but our feelings and perceptions about ourselves and the event are significantly altered.

Sometimes, as we simply confess and lift up feelings of pain, bitterness or fear, the Holy Spirit touches those places where the hurt resides, even when we have no specific memories about the source of that pain. The prophet Isaiah says: "Surely he took up our infirmities and carried our sorrows, yet we considered him stricken by God, smitten by him, and afflicted. But he was pierced for our transgressions, he was crushed for our iniquities; the punishment that brought us peace was upon him, and by his wounds we are healed." (Isa. 53:4-5)

The ongoing ministry of Jesus is a healing ministry, made possible by his sacrifice on the cross. The healing of bodies, hearts, minds and emotions are all part of his ongoing ministry through the Spirit. We should not be surprised when Jesus heals today for he is the same yesterday, today and forever. Jesus has promised to heal the brokenhearted and to bind up their wounds. He has promised that his truth will set us free. We simply come to him and ask him to do what he has promised. We may need to ask only once or we may need to pray on several occasions as he takes us through a process of healing.

Basic Process for Healing:

When you frequently experience deep emotional pain from normal interaction with other people, or when you continue to hold bitterness and resentment toward specific people from your past, it may be time to seek God for healing in those areas of your soul. You must trust him to lead you to those places needed for healing and trust him to be with you in those places. Familiarize yourself with this process. Later in the book, you will have the opportunity to experience the process.

- Spend quality time in prayer and worship. Reflect on God's promises for healing.
- Declare your trust in Jesus and ask him to take you to the birthplace of your brokenness. Ask him to be present with you in that memory. Ask him also to bind Satan and keep him from intruding into your experience with Jesus.
- As the Spirit of Christ takes you to a specific memory, reflect on the details, the emotions, the colors, the smells, the people involved, and what you were feeling about yourself or about God as you went through that experience.
- When you are solidly in that memory and in that moment...
    ◊ Ask Jesus where he was while you were being wounded.
    ◊ Ask Jesus to speak to you about that experience — the truth about what happened and the truth about you.
    ◊ See yourself as a child in that moment and ask Jesus the questions you have always wanted to ask. You may picture him in that moment or simply hear him.

Some memories are still very powerful and traumatic. I would encourage you to have a trusted friend with faith to pray with you as you revisit these memories and ask the Lord to join you. Jesus is faithful. He is willing to join you in the birthplace of the strongholds in your life. His desire is to set you free with his truth.

- Having heard the truth, test it in your spirit to see if it reflects the character of Jesus, the truth of scripture, and to see if it produced the fruit of peace in your heart. Then, ask the Spirit to write that truth on your heart so that you can never forget it.
- Finally, ask the Holy Spirit to take the painful emotions and lies that were sown through that experience and nail them to the cross of Jesus Christ. Ask him to fill you with the truth, peace and joy of Jesus, where the hurt once resided. Ask him to restore what was stolen from you (Joel 2:25).
- As you have heard from Jesus and asked the Holy Spirit to take away the pain and lies, renounce any negative or sinful desires and emotions and release them in the name of Jesus. Be sure to forgive those who have wounded you so that you give no further place to the enemy.

Jesus often surprises us as we take people through this process. Several years ago, I had been meeting with a young man named Mark who was overcome with shame about his secret homosexual life. He had been raised in a conservative Christian home but after being molested as a young man, he had found himself drawn powerfully to homosexual pornography. From time to time he had secret liaisons with other men he met online. None of his friends, family, or church knew anything of his struggle or his sin.

He had come in desperation for one last attempt to overcome this sin in his life. He was convinced that God hated him and had totally rejected him. He felt helpless to resist his impulses and was strongly committed to the idea that if something didn't happen quickly, he was going to give in to his impulses, abandon his family, and fully embrace a homosexual lifestyle.

On several occasions, Mark made the comment that if he could just believe that God didn't hate him, he might be able to hang on to his faith and family. I asked him if he was willing to let Jesus speak to him about his struggle. Mark was fearful of God's rebuke but willing to try. We simply prayed and asked

Jesus to come and tell Mark how he felt about him. In a moment, Mark burst into tears and began to weep, not quietly but uncontrollably.

After several minutes passed, I asked Mark what Jesus had spoken to him. He lifted his head and said that Jesus had really not spoken anything to him, but he clearly, physically felt the Lord embrace him with warmth and comfort. The touch of Jesus spoke more loudly than any words could have. Over the next few weeks, Mark heard from the Lord several times as Jesus confirmed his love and faith in Mark. Mark began to pray again, stand in faith again and noticed significant changes in his heart and attitude towards others. His anger toward his "molester" had diminished and he began to find joy in his life and work again. In his renewed relationship with Christ, Mark was managing his impulses to go online and to call "old friends."

After a few weeks, I began to speak to Mark about the possibility of deliverance. The whole idea of demonic affliction terrified Mark but soon he felt that God was pointing him in that direction. Two of us took Mark through a process of deliverance where we encountered marked manifestations, especially when we dealt with sexual spirits. Afterwards, though he was exhausted in the end, Mark knew something at his core had shifted — Jesus had set him free. The last time I had a conversation with Mark, he was continuing to walk in freedom and his life had changed radically. When God confirms his love in us in ways that we can truly believe, everything changes. That is what inner healing is truly about.

The following is an example of prayer for healing and freedom.

Lord Jesus, you know my emotional pain. You know the anger, fear and rejection that come up in me — prompting me to lash out at the people I love. Sometimes I cut myself off from them so that I cannot give love or receive love, as you desire. Lord Jesus, you have all authority in heaven and on earth. You are Lord over my past, my present and my future. You are my healer and you know the source of my pain. Will you now bring to mind any past experience I need to relive with you at my side for my healing? Lord, please take me to the birthplace of my painful emotions. [Search your memory for the experience in which you first remember feeling the emotions you are praying about. Go back until you stay in one experience.]

Lord Jesus, you were present when this happened to me. Will you now help me to remember this moment in detail? Allow me to unlock the feelings that I have covered up. Bring them out into the light for your truth and healing. Jesus, I trust you to open up my memories so that you can touch every part of that experience. [Now remember the details, the feelings, the people, the words spoken, and the conclusions you came to about yourself and about God.]

Lord Jesus, be present with me in that moment and tell me what you want me to know about what happened, about the people who did this to me, about me, and about you. Lord, help me see myself in that moment and speak your truth to me as the child I was then, so that I might put away a child's understanding by the power of your Spirit. [As the Lord speaks to you, test the spirit of the message to see if it is consistent with the character of Christ, lines up with Scripture, and creates peace in your heart. If so, move ahead.]

Holy Spirit, please write the truth of Jesus Christ on my heart so that I may know the truth and be set free from the lies of the enemy. I now lift up the lies I have believed, along with my anger, my bitterness, my fear and rejection and give them to you. Holy Spirit, I plead the blood of Christ over my wounds for healing and release these lies and this pain to you to be nailed to the cross. In the name of Jesus, I forgive those who wounded me and release them from the debt they owe. I entrust them to you Lord Jesus and ask that you bless them as you see fit. I now receive your truth, your joy, your peace, your love and your healing, in Jesus' name...Amen.

You may need to go to that painful memory several times, but always ask Jesus to go with you. You may need to revisit several experiences that produced lies and painful emotions through the years. Trust Jesus. Take him there. Ask him to heal your broken heart. James encourages us to "confess our faults one to another and pray for one another that we might be healed" (James 5:16). Sharing your burdens with trusted believers and allowing them to pray over you for healing is also a significant way through which Jesus ministers love and healing to his people.

Personal Reflection / Journaling:

Begin to acknowledge the unhealed wounds in your heart from past experiences. Although you were a victim when you received these wounds, you are now responsible for acknowledging them and seeking God's healing. You may no longer excuse your behavior, blame the past, or blame others when you withhold love, give in to rage, lie or medicate with your "drug of choice" (and so on). Consider the **Indicators of Unhealed Wounds** earlier in this chapter. Mark those that you recognize as having been a part of you.

Healing becomes a matter of obedience when we use our wounds to excuse our disobedience, continue in unforgiveness, deny personal responsibility for our sins, or limit our spiritual growth. If our "woundedness" has become our identity it may even be scary to ask God for healing since our emotional wound has organized our life for years. But Jesus has something better. He will organize your life and your identity is already in him. Ask God to show you any areas of your life where you have used your woundedness as an excuse for disobedience. Lift those attitudes and behaviors up to God in repentance and ask him to bring you to a place of healing and transformation.

Prayer Focus

If you are ready and can trust Jesus, you may want to revisit some of the places where painful emotions and lies were born. I recommend you ask someone to walk with you the first or second time you go through this process. "Confess your faults one to another and pray for one another that you may be healed." (James 5:16)

Pray for the Holy Spirit to begin to touch broken places inside of you with his truth and his healing power. Ask him to tear down strongholds that either you or the enemy has built up and to begin to set you free from lies that have hindered your freedom through the years. If you are not ready to address those issues, you may simply want to begin to identify patterns of emotional brokenness in your life that you may take to Jesus at a later time.

Memory Verse:

"But he was pierced for our transgressions, he was crushed for our iniquities; the punishment that brought us peace was upon him, and by his wounds we are healed." (Isa. 53:5)

Chapter Nine

AUTHORITY TO COMMAND

And you have been given fullness in Christ, who is the head over every power and authority. (Col. 2:10)

B elievers live under grace because the blood of Christ has set us free from the judgment and authority of law. However, the remainder of creation — seen and unseen — operates under law and law operates by power and authority. Because of that, Scripture highlights again and again the authority of Jesus Christ. That authority has also been delegated to those who follow Christ. Walking in that authority and exercising it in biblical ways is essential to freedom and healing. This chapter establishes the biblical framework for that authority and explores the exercise of that authority in setting captives free. Scripture emphasizes the authority of Christ over and over.

All authority in heaven and on earth has been given to me. (Matt. 28:18)

God raised Christ from the dead and seated him at his right hand in the heavenly realms, far above all rule and authority, power and dominion, and every title that can be given, not only in the present age but in the age to come. And God placed all things under his feet and appointed him head over everything for the Church. (Eph. 1:20-22)

Therefore, God has exalted him to the highest place and gave him the name that is above every name that at the name of Jesus every knee should bow in heaven and on earth and under the earth and every tongue confess that Jesus is Lord. (Phil. 2:9-11)

These verses and others confirm that Jesus has all authority and wields the power of heaven on behalf of his people. Notice in the Ephesians passage above that God placed everything under the feet of Jesus and appointed him head over everything *for* the Church. That small preposition means that the Father gave Jesus his position of ultimate power and authority on behalf of the Church and we are the Church. It is not God's intent that Jesus rule over his Church but that Jesus rule with his Church. Therefore, he empowers his Church on this earth to push back the enemy and continually expand the borders of the kingdom until he returns.

Christ has also delegated his authority to believers.

Throughout his ministry, Jesus demonstrated the power of the kingdom of heaven on earth. His pattern was simple and consistent. Preach the good news of the kingdom of heaven, heal the sick, raise the dead and cast out demons. He then sent out the twelve to "try their wings" without him. They were to go and do as he had been doing. Before sending them out, he called the twelve together and gave them power and authority to drive out demons and cure diseases (Matt. 10:1; Luke 9:1-2).

After sending out the twelve, Jesus sent out seventy-two other disciples to also emulate his ministry. "The seventy-two returned with joy and said, 'Lord, even the demons submit to us in your name." he replied, "I saw Satan fall like lightning from heaven. I have given you authority to trample on snakes and scorpions and to overcome all the power of the enemy; nothing will harm you. However, do not rejoice that the spirits submit to you, but rejoice that your names are written in heaven" (Luke 10:17-20).

Finally, Jesus delegated that same power and authority to all believers so that the Church could continue to carry out his ministry by the Spirit.

I tell you the truth, anyone who has faith in me will do what I have been doing. He will do even greater things than these because I am going to the Father. And I will do whatever you ask in my name, so that the Son may bring glory to the Father. (John 14:12-13)

And these signs will accompany those who believe: In my name they will drive out demons, they will speak in new tongues…they will place their hands on sick people, and they will get well. (Mark 16:17-18)

Jesus intended his ministry to continue through the church and through those who had faith in his name long after his ascension and the death of his apostles. This power is also seen through the gifts of the Holy Spirit discussed by Paul in 1 Corinthians and Romans. In those lists of spiritual gifts are prophecy, words of knowledge and wisdom, gifts of healing (which includes deliverance from demons), miraculous powers, and so forth.

In my early years as a follower of Jesus, I was taught that the miracles of Jesus, which for the most part were healing and deliverance, were granted only for a few years during the first century. These were given only as proofs of his claim to be the Son of God and the Messiah. The apostles were then given these miraculous powers as a kind of *seal of approval* for their declaration of the gospel in the name of Jesus and to establish their writings in the New Testament as inspired works of the Holy Spirit. Once the record of Christ's miracles was written and the New Testament penned, the "need for miracles" ceased and passed away as the last apostles died.

However, a quick review of the New Testament clearly shows that Jesus gave power and authority to preach, heal, and cast out demons to many others besides the twelve. In addition to the seventy- two, Stephen and Philip, as well as deacons in the Jerusalem church, all performed great signs and miracles as well (Acts 6:8; 8:13). The whole flavor of 1 Corinthians 12-14 is that supernatural gifts were distributed throughout the church.

Christ delegated authority personally and by the Holy Spirit so that his followers might continue to expand the borders of God's kingdom on earth. True disciples of any teacher learn to live as he lived and do what he did. They do not follow him daily so that they can just talk about the life they saw him lead as if they are reporters following a story. Jesus called his followers to reproduce his life.

Love one another as I have loved you. (John 13:34)

Now that I, your Lord and Teacher have washed your feet, you also should wash one another's feet. (John 13:14)

As the Father has sent me, I am sending you. (John 20:21)

Jesus told his disciples that they were to emulate his life. That's what disciples do. Whatever Jesus did, we are to do as well. And so, Jesus continues to give power and authority to overcome the enemy and to fulfill his mission statement expressed in Isaiah 61.

We must "line up under" Christ's authority if we are to minister with his authority.

When Jesus had entered Capernaum, a centurion came to him, asking for help. "Lord," he said, "my servant lies at home paralyzed and in terrible suffering." Jesus said to him, "I will go and heal him." The centurion replied, "Lord, I do not deserve to have you come under my roof. But just say the word, and my servant will be healed. For I myself am a man under authority, with soldiers under me. I tell this one, 'Go,' and he goes; and that one, 'Come,' and he comes. I say to my servant, 'Do this,' and he does it." When Jesus heard this, he was astonished and said to those following him, "I tell you the truth, I have not found anyone in Israel with such great faith...Then Jesus said to the centurion, "Go! It will be done just as you believed it would." And his servant was healed at that very hour. (Matt. 8:8-10, 13)

The Roman centurion, whose faith "astonished" Jesus, understood authority. The Roman army operated on strict lines of authority where commands were unquestioned. The centurion gave orders and they were obeyed immediately because he operated with the authority of Caesar himself. As long as the centurion received orders from his commanders and worked within the parameters of his rank, he had the power of the Roman military machine to enforce his commands if any enemy refused to obey. The centurion understood that Christ healed because he had authority in both the spiritual and physical realm. Our faith is connected to an understanding of his authority and our identity in him.

Faith is not just a belief that Jesus exists or that he is good and has made many amazing promises. Faith also is the certainty that he can and will fulfill those promises by his power and authority. Our Lord never has to say, "I'll see what I can do." On the contrary, "For no matter how many promises God has made, they are 'Yes' in Christ." (2 Cor. 1:20) Just as the centurion could command with authority because he was lined up under those with greater authority, the greater our alignment with Christ the greater the flow of his power and authority will be to us and through us. Think of yourself as a conduit or a pipeline of God's grace where his power first flows to you and then through you to others. When the conduit is clean and straight, the flow is maximized. If the conduit has bends, kinks, or debris within its walls, the flow is greatly hindered.

If the centurion had stepped out of the ranks, issuing orders that had not come down to him from above, he would have had no power but his own to enforce his commands. It is the same in the spiritual realm. When we are walking in relationship and obedience to the Lordship of Jesus, then we minister in his authority and the power and protection of heaven are available to us. When we are walking outside of his authority or his will, we make ourselves vulnerable to the enemy and operate in our own strength rather than in the strength of the King of Kings.

The city of God described in Revelation 21 has a "great high wall" around it. Think of God's protection as a great high wall surrounding us. The enemy can assault us and harass us from outside, but we are safe within the walls of Christ's protection. Un-repented sin, self-sufficiency, or areas in which we don't trust God become openings in the wall that may give the enemy access. Having gained entrance, he may establish himself firmly in our lives. Sometimes the opening is just a crack in the door. Sometimes the gates are thrown wide open. If we participate in the things of Satan, we invite him to take up residence with us because we have come into agreement with him. When Satan gains access to our lives, he will establish footholds that over time become strongholds. We experience these spiritual strongholds when we feel out of control or in bondage to something. The Apostle Paul gave us warnings about parts of our lives "un-surrendered" to Christ.

"Don't you know that when you offer yourselves to someone to obey him as slaves, you are slaves to the one whom you obey—whether you are slaves to sin, which leads to death, or to obedience, which leads to righteousness?" (Rom. 6:16)

"In your anger, do not sin. Do not let the sun go down while you are still angry, and do not give the devil a foothold." (Eph. 4:26)

In these verses, Paul tells us that un-surrendered segments of our lives make us vulnerable to the enemy. In the passage from Romans, Paul is clear that sin no longer has any legal claim on us but we can still enter into *voluntary servitude* to sin and become its slave again. By offering our bodies as instruments of wickedness, we come into agreement with Satan. By doing so, we open a door and invite the enemy into our house. Our sin gives him authority to oppress us. If sin isn't dealt with soon, Satan will gain a foothold that will soon becomes a stronghold. Addictions are the perfect example of this process. A little taste, a little look, a little indulgence that is not acknowledged, confessed and placed at the foot of the cross, and it calls to us again and again. At first we can walk away but eventually we become slaves by our own choices.

Out of Alignment

If we want to experience the fullness of Christ, we must stay in alignment with his ways and his will. However, there are other forces tugging on us and attempting to change our direction. The prophet Amos declared, "Can two walk together accept they be agree" (Amos 3:3, KJV)? If two people have different destinations, they cannot walk together for long. Soon they will separate and go their own ways. Satan's ploy is to separate our purposes from the purposes of Jesus little by little. Only one degree of separation will remove us from one another by miles if we walk that direction long enough. Self-examination, confession and repentance are constant course corrections that keep us walking with Jesus. Being aware of the things that call us in a different direction helps us to avoid being out of alignment with him.

Sources of Temptation

There are three sources of temptation that hinder our walk with Christ and the freedom that is available in him: our flesh, the world, and demonic activity:

Our Flesh

The *flesh* is our *fallen nature* or the *natural man*. It includes a physical body that is subject to death and decay. It also includes a soul that is self-centered and rebellious — wanting its own way in everything. We inherited both from Adam. The Apostle Paul characterizes this desire as an active force that dwells in our flesh actively prompting us to rebel against God while demanding its own way.

> I do not understand what I do. For what I want to do I do not do, but what I hate I do…As it is, it is no longer I myself who do it, but it is sin living in me…For I have the desire to do what is good, but I cannot carry it out. For what I do is not the good I want to do; no the evil I do not want to do — this I keep on doing. Now if I do what I do not want to do, it is no longer I who do it, but it is sin living in me that does it… (Rom. 7:15-20)

The flesh is a two year old lying on the floor, kicking and screaming and demanding immediate gratification. The body is not inherently evil. It is God's creation and within it are godly desires as well as evil desires. When Adam sinned, however, something was corrupted within our natural man. The soul (intellect, emotions and will) began to rule over the spirit rather than the spirit ruling over the soul. Unfortunately, the flesh will always be with us until we receive our glorified bodies at the resurrection. And yet we can strengthen the spirit and weaken the flesh so that its influence in our lives becomes less and less.

There are several keys to overcoming the flesh and maintaining your alignment with God:

- **Agree with God about sin and the sin in your life.**
  Agree that God's standards are right and just. When you break his standards, view it as sin and call it sin rather than adopting society's view and language which excuses the wrong attitude or action.
- **Acknowledge the sin by confessing it and your responsibility in choosing the sin.**
  Do not excuse it, minimize it, justify it or blame others. God is quick to forgive when we acknowledge the sin and have godly sorrow about it — a sorrow that comes from wanting to please the God we love.

- **Receive God's truth that you do not have to submit to sin. You can choose to say "no" to sin through the power of Christ.**

  "You, however, are controlled not by the sinful nature but by the Spirit if the Spirit of God lives in you." (Rom. 8:9) As a believer, the sinful nature tempts you but does not have a legal claim on you, nor does it ultimately control you. You are free in Christ to choose righteousness. As soon as we begin to think, "we can't help it," we have voluntarily given control to sin. On the contrary, we can do all things through Christ who strengthens us (Phil. 4:13). Therefore, declare your strength in him rather than declaring your weakness.

- **Repent of the sin.**

  Repentance is literally a change of mind. When we have not been in agreement with God but then choose to align our thoughts and behaviors with him, we have repented. Coming into agreement with God about sin and committing to overcome it with his help (not just in your mind but also in your heart), is an essential step in gaining freedom over any sin. Often sin is prompted by a desire to meet an emotional need that we have not trusted God to meet. Repentance there is not just rejecting our sinful behavior but beginning to trust God to meet a legitimate need in a righteous way.

  Another key to turning away from sin at a heart level is to project what will happen when the sin runs its course. Ask Jesus to show you the end of the matter if you continue in the sin. Deception keeps us in the moment of a fantasy about what a particular sin will do for us. But ask Jesus to show you the outcome of the fantasy. Seeing past the moment to the end of the scenario when sin destroys us or the ones we love is a strong motivation for repentance.

- **Continue to receive God's forgiveness by faith based on the sacrifice of Jesus Christ.**

  If we confess our sins, he is faithful and just and will forgive us our sins and purify us from all unrighteousness. (1 John 1:9)

It is imperative that we remember that the blood of God's Son has purchased the forgiveness of our sins past, present and future. Satan loves to whisper in the ear of every believer that we were initially saved by grace because we didn't know any better. But now that we know God's will, his forgiveness is not so available. It may come to us but only after we have beaten ourselves up enough or until God has punished us like an angry father.

The "angry father view" is a false view of God. God has already punished our sin through Jesus. Jesus has taken care of our sin problem as long as we still have a heart for him...and by that I don't mean a perfect heart. We were saved by grace and we continue by grace. Monitoring our lives for sin and bringing those sins to the Father so that they are clearly submitted to the cross, keeps sin from gaining ground in our lives and prevents Satan from gaining a foothold.

It is the secret sin and the unacknowledged sin that have the most power in our lives. It is through those sins that Satan finds a way to take stake out a piece of territory in us. Constant confession is a way of weeding the garden while the weeds are still small. Living with confidence in the readiness of God to forgive is essential to bringing every sin and weakness before him so that each is continually washed away by the blood of Christ.

- **Quickly extend forgiveness to others who have wronged or wounded you.**

  For if you forgive men when they sin against you, your heavenly Father will also forgive you. (Matt. 6:14)

  A refusal to forgive others hinders our relationship with God in significant ways and opens the door to satanic influence. Unforgiveness is the seed of bitterness, judgment, vengeance, gossip, slander and a host of other behaviors and attitudes that create distance between our hearts and God's heart. Forgiveness is not an option for the believer. We can forgive from a distance if the one who has wronged us will wrong us again if given the opportunity.

- **Feed the Spirit and starve the flesh.**

  Within every believer live the "spiritual man" who loves God and the "natural man" who resists God. The one you feed the most will be the stronger. The one you starve the most will be the weaker. We choose what we watch, read, do, and allow ourselves to think about. We choose our companions, our vocations, and our entertainment. Through those choices we feed one and starve the other.

- **Invite accountability and prayer when you struggle.**

  "Confess your sins one to another and pray for one another that you may be healed." (James 5:16) Scripture encourages us to have some people in our lives with whom we can be honest about our spiritual struggles. We all need prayer. We all need encouragement. We all need another set of eyes on our life to keep us from deception. Every great athlete needs a coach to see what the athlete can't see, to encourage him to take one more lap, and to cheer him on when he is pushing toward the finish. We need people in our spiritual lives to do the same.

- **Store up God's Word in your heart.**
"I have hidden your word in my heart, that I might not sin against you" (Ps. 119:11). Jesus promised that the Holy Spirit would lead us into all truth and remind us of what Jesus had already taught us. The Holy Spirit is faithful to bring God's Word to mind in situations where you need to be reminded of God's will for you or reminded of a promise on which you can stand. Study, meditation, and memorization place that word in your heart for the Holy Spirit to draw from when you need to hear God the most.

- **Pray for strength to say "no" to your flesh.**
"Pray that you will not fall into temptation" (Luke 22:40). Don't assume that you will overcome the flesh in your own strength. Even Jesus spent entire nights in prayer seeking strength to say "no" to the flesh, the world and the enemy. Pray on all occasions and ask others to pray for you.

The World

In Scripture, "the world" sometimes refers to the people who live in this world and the creation as God intended it. *"For God so loved the world that he gave his one and only Son."* (John 3:16) At other times, "the world" refers to the systems of thought and values that oppose God — the systems that are ruled by the "prince of this world." (John 14:30) The Apostle John tells us, "Do not love the world or anything in the world." (1 John 2:15)

The *world,* in this context is the world's distorted systems of religion, art, science, media, education, and government that shout to us constantly, seeking to draw us away from God's truth and his ways. This is not to say that art, education, science, media and government are inherently evil. These are all meant to be expressions of the mind of God on this planet and can be used for great good. But to an alarming extent, Satan has co-opted and corrupted these systems for his purposes. They constantly point us to sources of security and significance other than God. They are used to "normalize" or even call good those things that God calls evil. The world then, in this sense, tempts us, seduces us, and calls us away from the things and values of God. Be careful of the things the world uses to call you away from the heart of God.

The Demonic

Sometimes, when we begin to discuss the demonic, we are tempted to see everything through the lens of demonic attack or affliction. Many times we are in bondage to sin because we have not chosen to resist it, crucify the flesh, feed the spiritual man or starve the natural man. We can spend a great deal of time trying to cast out a spirit when the flesh is the issue. Even when a spirit is involved, it is usually just magnifying what is already in the flesh. When deliverance is indicated and spirits are cast out, the newly freed individual will still have to deal with the temptation of the flesh, although the power and compulsion of the temptation will be greatly diminished. Having said that, demonic spirits are a very real issue — even for believers.

Demonic spirits are a given in Scripture. Their origins are not explained. There are numerous theories about their origins but each seems to fall short in some regard. God chose not to spell out their origins but he has been very clear about their existence and activity. They are mentioned in the Old Testament as spirits related to idol worship, especially involving human sacrifice.

> They made him jealous with their foreign gods and angered him with their detestable idols. They sacrificed to demons, which are not God— gods they had not known, gods that recently appeared, gods your fathers did not fear. (Deut. 32:16-17)

As soon as we begin to read through the pages of the gospels, there seems to be a very developed view of demons and their activity in Israel. Many come to Jesus or his disciples specifically seeking deliverance from demons and most seem to have an accurate view when unclean spirits are the source of torment in a person.

> News about him spread all over Syria, and people brought to him all who were ill with various diseases, those suffering severe pain, the demon-possessed, those having seizures, and the paralyzed, and he healed them. (Matt. 4:24)

There are dozens of accounts of deliverance in the gospels. Some experienced these spirits as mental and emotional anguish such as the man "of the Gadarenes" who lived among the tombs, crying out day and night and cutting himself (Mark 5:1ff). Others experienced some bondage as a strong, persistent compulsion to sin. We are told that Jesus cast seven demons out of Mary Magdalene. Church tradition suggests that she had been a prostitute before becoming a follower of Jesus.

Others experienced unclean spirits as sickness or a physiological condition. Among the physiological manifestations of demons recorded in the New Testament are blindness, deafness, muteness, convulsions, chronic back problems and so on. The writers of the gospels clearly differentiate between those who were ill, diseased, and physiologically impaired and those who were demonized. Often these demons mimicked disease and physiological problems but the writers knew the difference.

Throughout the gospels, Jesus and his followers demonstrated power and authority over Satan and his representatives. John tells us that Jesus came to destroy the works of the devil (1 John 3:8). Those works were the lies that Satan had sown in the earth, the power of sin, disease, physical impairment, demonic oppression and ultimately death. Jesus answered each one of those satanic strongholds with his presence, his power and his prayer, "Your kingdom come, your will be done on earth as it is in heaven" (Matt. 6:10).

In his ministry, Jesus consistently preached the good news of the Kingdom of God, healed the sick, raised the dead and cast out demons. Jesus and his followers demonstrated the authority of Christ over these spirits. Believers today have that same authority in Christ.

Some maintain that followers of Jesus cannot be oppressed by demons because we belong to Jesus and have been purchased by his blood. It is true that Satan cannot **possess** a believer because we have been purchased by Christ and are his possession. However, we can be afflicted, hindered, and harassed by demons in the same way that those who belong to Christ can still be in bondage to sin, illness and a multitude of addictions.

Many believers come to the Lord with demons already active in their lives from years of sin. Many come with demons that have been passed down through generations of their family. When they declare faith in Christ, they cross over the river into the promises of God. But, there is still the enemy that possessed pockets of the land before this believer came to faith and the enemy may still need to be rooted out by divine weapons.

We understand this principle when it comes to sin. Rising from the waters of baptism gives us a sinless position in Christ but not a sinless condition. The Holy Spirit dwells in us, but must share space with those things that are offensive to him while we mature. Jesus dwells in our heart, but sin also dwells there as we engage in the process of sanctification. Believers are not immune from falling into new expressions of sin and even bondage long after they have come to know Jesus. It is no different with the demonic. We can bring them into the kingdom with us or we can open the door of our own house and give them a place after we have entered the kingdom.

I have seen hundreds of people delivered from demons. Many had been oppressed by these demons from childhood as they were subjected to abuse of all kinds, occult activities and other trauma. Many were in bondage to sexual sin or drugs since their teen years. Nearly all of these individuals who experienced life-changing freedom in the name of Jesus were believers. We possess salvation through Christ and all his promises are ours...yet we may still need to drive the enemy out of territory that was once his. We must also live aligned with Christ so that the enemy has no point of entrance into our lives and so that we do not becomes slave to sin again voluntarily. If we were not vulnerable to the enemy, we would not need the armor of God nor divine weapons.

Demons attack individuals through temptation, harassment or torment. Many come and lay siege to us for a while but then move on. Others, however, afflict or oppress individuals (even believers) by attaching themselves to that individual — even for a lifetime. These oppressive spirits constantly influence the individual's thinking, emotions, and decision-making. Where curses have been established in a person's life, demons are assigned to enforce the directives of the curse.

As believers, Satan only has as much authority in our lives as we give him. The cross has taken away the legal claim that Satan had over us based on the law of sin and death. After coming to Christ, we still exercise our free will. Many believers still choose to walk in rebellion, dabble in the occult, nurture a secret sin, and so forth. By doing so, these believers give Satan a legal right to access them and their families.

Renting Out a Room

> When an evil spirit comes out of a man, it goes through arid places seeking rest and does not find it. Then it says, 'I will return to the house I left.' When it arrives, it finds the house swept clean and put in order. Then it goes and takes seven other spirits more wickedly than itself, and they go in and live there. And the final condition of that man is worse than the first. (Luke 11:24-26)

Think of it this way. Jesus spoke of our bodies as if they were houses where unclean spirits might reside. Demonic affliction for a believer is like renting out a room to a boarder. When you initially meet the boarder, he seems nice enough. He promises to be quiet, rarely has friends over, and has the lights out by 10 p.m. every night. And so, you sign a lease allowing him to stay. You take him at his word and add no clauses to the contract regarding noise, lights out, cooking in his room, or anything else. Your new boarder seems like "good folks" and so you welcome him in.

Shortly after your renter moves in, however, you begin to notice the music is a little loud, strange odors drift through your house, lights don't go out at 10 p.m., but loud friends stay until sunrise nearly every night. Feeling betrayed, you remind him of his verbal commitments and tell him sternly that if the noise and odors don't stop you will demand that he move out. Your renter simply looks at you with a smirk and laughs and, showing you the lease you signed, he declares, "I have a perpetual lease that you signed. None of the conditions you mentioned appear on our contract. I'm not going anywhere!" With that, he turns, closes the door to his room, and turns up his music.

He doesn't own your house or control what goes on in the remainder of your home, but he is there, harassing, tormenting and disturbing you as he chooses. He has a legal right to reside in your house and will do what he can to disrupt your life until you find a way to revoke his lease and have him escorted from your property. Demonic spirits can establish footholds and strongholds in the life of a believer if given a "legal" right to be present.

A believer can be afflicted by an oppressive spirit when...

- The believer has served sin or is serving sin for extended periods without confession or repentance. Walking in agreement with the enemy gives him access.

- There is a failure to forgive those who have wronged us. Unforgiveness is a huge door through which the enemy can enter our lives and take up residence. Satan gains access to us through our attitudes that are contrary to the mind of Christ. Unless we forgive others, God does not forgive us. Unforgiven sin is an open door.

- Those who have had authority over a person have served sin. Exodus 20 tells us that the sins of the fathers will be visited upon the children to the third and fourth generation. The consequences of un-repented sin may be passed down to the children. If the consequence of the sin has been demonic oppression, then that consequence is also passed on to the children.

  Husbands, who demand that their wives participate in sin with them (pornography, group sex, occult activities, etc.), can also be a conduit for demonic oppression over their wives.

- A person has experienced trauma...especially violent or sexual trauma. Trauma may give demonic spirits access through the pain, the shame or the fear created by the trauma. Often, the trauma does not open the person up but the anger, bitterness, and unforgiveness held by the wounded person toward those who hurt him makes him vulnerable to the enemy as well.

- Curses, judgments or vows have been spoken against the person. Curses, judgments, and vows give Satan legal access to us so that demonic spirits may be assigned to enforce the words that have been declared. We will discuss this truth in detail later.

The believer is not possessed but rather *oppressed* or *afflicted* by such spirits. The idea of demon possession is misleading for the most part. Possession suggests that demon(s) are in total control of a person. The Gadarene demoniac who lived among the tombs and was inhabited by Legion probably falls under that category. The Manson's, the Hitler's, and Dahmer's of the world are most likely possessed.

For the most part, however, individuals will experience demonic oppression as a bondage in part of their life and one in which they can still sometimes exercise control. The remainder of their life will have normalcy to it, even to the extent that others who know them may be unaware of their bondage. Yet, the bondage torments them with secrecy and shame and greatly hinders their relationship with the Father. The good news of the Kingdom of God, however, is that the authority of Christ is sufficient to set us free from demons when we trust him, submit ourselves to his authority, and bring our lives into alignment with him.

Freedom from the World, the Flesh and the Demonic

Freedom from the world means that the environment does not draw us away from Christ. Jesus said that we will be "in the world," but should not be "of the world" (John 17:15-16). Submitting our environment to Christ means saying "no" to influences that compromise our walk with the Lord. These may include...

- Some relationships that influence us and cause us to compromise our faith. Paul warns us not be "yoked together with unbelievers." The idea of a yoke is influence or some kind of binding covenant. Even Solomon fell to the influence of relationships with unbelievers.
- Employment that requires us to participate in activities that strengthen the flesh and starve the spirit, or that cause us to compromise our Christian values. It may just be a group of co-workers who love to party and enjoy happy hour every afternoon. It may be an office full of gossip, backbiting and sexual immorality. A mature Christian may choose to stay in such an environment as a witness and as a mission, but most believers are pulled down by such environments as the environment constantly feeds and reinforces the flesh, while the spirit goes begging.
- Input from the world such as media, literature, and music that glorifies and normalizes sin.

Idols are offered by the world as substitutes for God. Whatever the world offers as an ultimate source of significance, identity, security, immortality, etc. is an idol. The enticement is not always sin in itself but it is devotion to things that are not eternal. Career, education, recreation, even family can hold a person's devotion over God and weaken our spiritual life.

Freedom from the flesh means that we have strengthened the spiritual man and weakened the natural man to the extent that certain ways of thinking and acting have been eradicated or weakened to the point that our resistance to them is not a daily battle of " just keeping the lid" on those thoughts or behaviors. Instead, we have real freedom so that when we resist with the divine weapons God has provided, the temptation loses its power and is consistently overcome.

Personal time in the Word, confession, repentance, prayer, praise, meditation and fellowship with other believers bring us into the presence of God on a regular basis so that his Spirit can change us and his Word can renew us. Feeding our spirit through communion with his Spirit and starving the flesh is the key.

Freedom from the demonic means that we have been set free from any bondage we suffer due to *demonic oppression* in our lives. Demons will still come to tempt us and attack from the outside. That is not a comforting thought until you remember that to wake up in the middle of the night hearing someone trying to get into your house is much better than waking up to realize they are already inside. If they are outside they can usually be turned away by turning on the lights or calling for help. If they are inside, it becomes much more complicated.

Tempters on the outside come and go. James tells us, "Resist the devil and he will flee from you" (James 4:7). They will come along, but resist them and they will depart. Put on the armor of God and stand. The blood of Christ and the authority of Christ are quite sufficient to keep us free when we submit all that we have to him. When we consistently reject the world, say "no" to the flesh, feed the spirit in the presence of God, and wield his divine weapons, we can walk in the freedom of Jesus Christ. If we find ourselves oppressed by the enemy or fighting strongholds within, Christ can still set us free for he has all authority in heaven and on earth. We will talk more about that in the chapter on deliverance.

Personal Reflection / Journaling —
A Critical Self Assessment

This is a critical step in finding freedom from the things that have held you in bondage. Again, the sources of the things that hinder us are the world, the flesh and the demonic. That realm also includes lies of the enemy established in our hearts, curses, soul ties, and demonic oppression. All of these will be discussed in detail in the next two chapters.

A thorough and honest inventory will be needed so that you may submit every part of your life to the blood and the Lordship of Jesus. Please be prayerful and thorough as you take stock of your spiritual condition.

Spiritual Self-Assessment
The World

"Search me, O God, and know my heart; test me and know my anxious thoughts. See if there is any offensive way in me, and lead me in the way everlasting." (Ps. 139:23-24)

What parts of your **environment** are outside of God's will for your life? What draws you away from the character of God and away from Jesus Christ being formed in you? What do you involve yourself in that is offensive to the Spirit of God? Which spiritually negative influences have you continued to love and not yet submitted to Jesus?

What relationships are you currently involved in that have a negative spiritual influence on you or that compromise your faith? Ask God to show you the truth about those relationships. Write them down or describe them below.

What activities do you participate in that the Spirit has urged you to give up? What actions will you take to be obedient?

What other things, people or priorities have you put before your relationship with God? Which of these things have you trusted more than God to give you significance, security, identity or fulfillment in your life?

What career requirements cause you to compromise some of the values of your faith? How can you respond to that?

What recreational activities have you given a higher priority than you should? How have they caused you to compromise biblical priorities or values?

What forms of media — movies, television, music, magazines, movies, games, etc. — do you look at or listen to that feeds the flesh rather than the spirit? What are you doing to feed your spirit?

The Flesh:

> Those who live according to the sinful nature have their minds set on what that nature desires; but those who live in accordance with the Spirit have their minds set on what the Spirit desires. (Rom. 8:5)

There are parts of our lives that are submitted to the desires of the Spirit, but there are almost always other parts that are not yet submitted. To find freedom, we need to acknowledge these areas where the sinful nature or the natural man still rules and submit them to the cross of Christ.

In what areas of the flesh (sinful nature) do you continue to struggle? Over what sinful thoughts or behaviors have you not yet gained victory?

_____Areas of sexual immorality — Adultery, fornication, sexual fantasy, pornography, homosexuality, sexual addiction, prostitution, etc.

_____Idolatry — Putting things before God. Seeking your significance, security, purpose, self-esteem, etc. from sources other than God.

_____Witchcraft — Involvement in false religion and occult practices in an effort to control your life or the lives of others (fortune-telling, Tarot cards, Ouija boards, horoscopes, Free Masonry, religious cults, white magic, black magic, satanic cults, etc.)

_____ Hatred, anger, jealousy, rage, envy, bitterness, resentment, revenge, unforgiveness, gossip, slander.

_____ Addictions — Drugs, alcohol, pornography, other sexual addictions, food, people pleasing, video games, television, computers, exercise, work, etc. Anything you have become dependent upon for a sense of well-being, comfort, significance, or dealing with emotional pain outside of Jesus Christ.

_____ Pride, arrogance, self-righteousness, a judgmental spirit, prejudice, bigotry.

_____ Rebellion

_____ Greed, envy, jealousy, covetousness, materialism.

_____ Other sins of the flesh that God has shown you.

Unforgiveness

Before receiving the forgiveness of Christ for the sins you have not yet surrendered to the cross, you must be obedient in the area of granting forgiveness. Forgiveness nullifies the legal right of Satan to oppress you, sets you free from the power of sin, and opens the door for intimate fellowship with Jesus. Determine if there is anyone who has wronged you or wounded you in the past that you have not forgiven. Be honest. Look for even small pockets of resentment and bitterness in your heart. Seek out anger and thoughts of revenge. Acknowledge these thoughts and feelings and list below any and everyone you still need to forgive.

Having identified the temptations of the world that are overcoming your spirit, the sins of the flesh over which you have not yet had victory, and any unforgiveness in your heart, now ask God to show you anything else that is hindering your freedom in Christ.

Receiving God's Forgiveness

After taking an inventory of your life, you may feel the weight of your imperfections. Often, the way we choose to deal with sin in our life is to not think about it at all. When we begin to assess our lives fully, we may become acutely aware of how many ways we fall short of God's standards. Having become aware, we may feel condemned under the load of our imperfections. At this point we simply need to take God at his word.

> If we claim to be without sin, we deceive ourselves and the truth is not in us. If we confess our sins, he is faithful and just and will forgive us our sins and purify us from all unrighteousness. (1 John 1:8-9)

> Therefore, there is now no condemnation for those who are in Christ Jesus. (Rom. 8:1)

God is quick to forgive when we align our hearts with his through confession and repentance. His forgiveness cannot to be earned by good works or self-loathing. It is a gift of grace. It takes faith to believe that God will forgive us just because we acknowledge our sin before him. But there comes a time when we need to receive God's full forgiveness by faith. When we have done what God has asked us to do regarding our sin, then we should declare our forgiveness whether we "feel forgiven" or not. God cannot lie so we can take him at his word. When we have done the following, we may declare our forgiveness in Jesus Christ.

Believe:
- Acknowledge that Jesus died for your sins and that his blood is sufficient payment for all your sin: past, present and future.

Confess:
- Acknowledge your sin — specifically if possible.
- Take personal responsibility for your sin — do not excuse, minimize, justify, or blame.
- Acknowledge God's standard as true and just.

Repent:
- Renounce your sin in the name of Jesus.
- Make a sincere commitment to turn from your sinful behaviors and thoughts and submit your actions and thoughts to the righteousness of Christ.

Forgive:
- Name those you have not forgiven and declare that forgiveness in the name of Jesus.

- Release all judgment to God.
- Renounce any hatred, unforgiveness, bitterness, resentment or thoughts of revenge you have held toward those individuals asking God to forgive you as you are forgiving those who hurt you.
- Pray a blessing over those individuals.
- Plead the blood of Christ over your heart and over those relationships, asking God to seal your heart so that the enemy cannot raise up unforgiveness in you again.

Receive
- By faith in the blood of Christ and the promises of God, receive the forgiveness that you have in Christ and give him thanks for the forgiveness he has granted.
- Stand on the promise that you are totally forgiven in Christ and that there is no condemnation for those who are in him.

Note: Walk in Forgiveness
If old feelings or thoughts related to unforgiveness arise in you, go through the same process I have just described and submit your heart, your mind, and those relationships to Jesus.

Prayer for Forgiveness
Now, having taken a thorough inventory of your life and having identified areas that you need to submit to the blood of Christ, pray over your sin and any area of unforgiveness as indicated above. You may want to pray over a few of these issues each night. Ask God to reveal anything further that needs to be laid at the foot of the cross. Remember, you are aligning yourself with the Lord and nullifying and legal claim the enemy has held against you. You may use the following models for your prayers.

Prayer to Forgive Others So That God Can Forgive You.
Heavenly Father, in the name of Jesus I forgive (name the person)
_____ *for the wrongs done to me. I forgive him/her for (the wrongs done to you)*

_____

In the name of Jesus I freely release all who have wronged me them from their debt. I lay nothing to their charge and release them to you for your righteous judgment. I do this in recognition of the debt I owed to you that I could never repay and in recognition of the fact that you totally forgave my debt, through your Son. I ask that you bless those whom I have forgiven as you see fit. In the name of Jesus and by his blood, I now cancel any legal claim that the enemy may have had against me because of my unforgiveness. Lord, strengthen me in my spirit that I may walk in this forgiveness I the days ahead. I ask these things and declare these things in Jesus' name...Amen.

Prayer for the Forgiveness of Your Sins

Heavenly Father, in the name of Jesus, I confess my sin and my rebellion before you. I have willfully chosen to rebel against you and your Word.

Specifically, I confess (sins) _____ and acknowledge that your standards are holy and just.

I have chosen to think and act in ways contrary to your will and your Word. I have no excuse and no one to blame — I have sinned against you. In the name of Jesus, I now renounce all my sins and my rebellion. There is nothing I can do to pay the debt of my sin and so by faith, I plead the blood of Jesus over that sin. Your Word declares that when I confess my sin, you will be faithful and just to forgive my sin and purify me from all unrighteousness. Your Word declares that in Christ, sin will not have dominion over me and I now come into agreement with your Word.

I now turn away from my sins and stand by the power of the cross through which I am crucified to the world, and the world is crucified to me. By your grace and by the blood of Christ, I am now dead to this sin. From this day forward, with your power, I will walk in freedom, no longer submitting to sin but to the righteousness of Christ.

I now receive your promise of forgiveness by faith and give you thanks. I praise you for your love and your mercy. Your Word declares that in Christ there is no condemnation and so I renounce the condemnation that the enemy would speak against me and I declare that I am now free in Christ from my sin. I now receive my forgiveness in Jesus' name...Amen.

Personal Reflection / Journaling:

What did God show you or speak to you through this process of self-examination, repentance, and forgiveness? Write down anything he spoke to you or revealed to you.

Suggested Memory Verse:

"There is, therefore, now no condemnation for those who are in Christ Jesus because through Christ Jesus, the law of the Spirit of life set me free from the law of sin and death." (Rom. 8:1-2)

Chapter Ten

CURSES!

But God said to Balaam, "Do not go with them. You must not put a curse on those people, because they are blessed." (Num. 22:12)

In this chapter, I am going to introduce the concept of curses. For many of us, when we think of curses, what comes to mind is superstition and old wives' tales. They seem like irrational notions that belong to another century. But Scripture disagrees and teaches us that curses can be a major hindrance to our freedom and healing. Again, however, the good news is that Christ provides the means to nullify any curses that have been operating in your life or your family.

A curse is an authoritative word spoken against a party that has the power to produce negative consequences in the life of the individual to whom it is assigned. Biblically, curses mobilize forces in the spiritual realm to affect the natural realm in ways that fulfill the curse for a season or for generations. A curse may be the consequence assigned to a sin or the result of specific words spoken over a particular individual by others (or by himself) that mobilizes forces in the spiritual realm.

Curse or a form of the word appears over 200 times in scripture. The word is first used in Genesis 3 although the concept is found as early as Genesis

2, when God tells Adam that eating from the tree of the knowledge of good and evil would produce death. Lastly, we find the concept in Revelation 22 when God warns that if anyone adds to or takes away from the words of that book, curses will fall upon him or her.

Most often, curses are a generic consequence assigned to a particular sin. God has established laws of reciprocity or inevitable consequences in both the natural and spiritual realm. It is the law of "sowing and reaping." Paul tells us, "The one who sows to please his sinful nature, from that nature will reap destruction; the one who sows to please the Spirit, from the Spirit will reap eternal life." (Gal. 6:8)

In the spiritual realm, God promises blessing for those who seek him. He also warns of curses for those who do not. Those who align themselves with God will experience good because God is good. Those who align themselves with Satan will experience destructive consequences because Satan is the destroyer.

In speaking to Abraham, God said, "I will bless those who bless you, and whoever curses you I will curse; and all peoples on earth will be blessed through you." (Gen. 12:3) Curses come to us when God turns us over to the established consequences of our own decisions. In Deuteronomy 27, God lists a host of blessings (life-giving consequences) for those who serve him faithfully and a host of curses (destructive consequences) for those who reject him or refuse to follow his ways. Other curses attached to certain sins are also found throughout the Bible.

It is important to note that these curses are not God taking his anger out on people who offend him. They are redemptive acts designed to restrain sin and turn people away from destruction. To do less would be to enable and reinforce sin assuring eternal punishment for even more than those who will demand hell, regardless of what God does to draw them to himself for, "God desires that all men should be saved" (1 Tim. 2:4).

Sins with Curses Attached

The following is a summary of the causes of curses as declared by God.

1. **Idolatry and False Worship**

   You shall not make for yourself an idol in the form of anything in heaven above or on the earth beneath or in the waters below. You shall not bow down to them or worship them; for I, the LORD your God, am a jealous God, punishing the children for the sin of the fathers to the third and fourth generation of those who hate me, but showing love to a thousand generations of those who love me and keep my commandments. (Deut. 5:8-10)

2. **Dishonoring Parents**

Cursed is the man who dishonors his father or his mother. (Deut. 27:16)

3. **Dishonesty, Injustice, and Violence (including abortion)**

Cursed is the man who moves his neighbor's boundary stone…Cursed is the man who leads the blind astray on the road…Cursed is the man who withholds justice from the alien, the fatherless or the widow. (Deut. 27:17-19)

Cursed is the man who kills his neighbor secretly… Cursed is the man who accepts a bribe to kill an innocent person. (Deut. 27:24-25)

4. **Sexual Immorality, Incest and Perversion**

Cursed is the man who sleeps with his father's wife, for he dishonors his father's bed…Cursed is the man who has sexual relations with any animal…Cursed is the man who sleeps with his sister, the daughter of his father or the daughter of his mother…Cursed is the man who sleeps with his mother-in-law. (Deut. 27:20-23)

5. **Spoken Curses by Self or Others**

He loved to pronounce a curse — may it come on him; he found no pleasure in blessing — may it be far from him. He wore cursing as his garment; it entered into his body like water, into his bones like oil. May it be like a cloak wrapped about him, like a belt tied forever around him. May this be the Lord's payment to my accusers, to those who speak evil of me. (Ps. 109:17-20)

6. **Robbing God**

Will a man rob God? Yet you rob me. But you ask, 'How do we rob you?' In tithes and offerings. You are under a curse — the whole nation of you — because you are robbing me. (Mal. 3:8, 9)

7. **Anti-Semitism**

In speaking to Abraham, God said, 'I will bless those who bless you, and whoever curses you I will curse.' (Gen. 12:3)

8. **Ignoring the Poor**

He who gives to the poor will lack nothing, but he who closes his eyes to them receives many curses. (Prov. 28:27)

9. **Trusting in Man Rather Than God**
   This is what the Lord says: Cursed is the one who trusts in man, who depends on flesh for his strength and whose heart turns away from the Lord. (Jer. 17:5)
10. **Refusing to Honor God**
    'If you do not listen, and if you do not set your heart to honor my name,' says the Lord Almighty, 'I will send a curse upon you, and I will curse your blessings.' (Mal. 2:2)

Generational Curses

Not only are those who commit these sins liable for the attached curses, but their descendants are liable as well. The Scriptures speak in numerous places of the sins of one generation adversely affecting future generations down to the third, fourth, even the tenth generation "of those who hate" God.

> You shall not bow down to them or worship them; for I, the Lord your God, am a jealous God, punishing the children for the sin of the fathers to the third and fourth generation of those who hate me. (Exodus 20:5)

> No one born of a forbidden marriage nor any of his descendants may enter the assembly of the LORD, even down to the tenth generation. (Deut. 23:2)

> If you do not carefully follow all the words of the law, which are written in this book, and do not revere this glorious and awesome name—the LORD your God—the LORD will send fearful plagues on you and your descendants, harsh and prolonged disasters, and severe and lingering illnesses. (Deut. 28:58-59)

The idea of one person being held responsible for what another has done is almost unthinkable in our culture. As Americans, we see ourselves as individuals, acting independently rather than acting as part of a family, a group, or a community that will also experience the consequences of our actions. Our perspective on individualism is such that we believe that what we do is our own concern and is no one else's business. As an extension of that thinking, we also believe that no one else should be held accountable for what we do, nor should we be held accountable for what someone else has done. The truth is that not only do I reap what I sow but also those attached to me reap what I sow. Families reap what their fathers sow. Nations reap what their leaders sow.

During the reign of King David there was a famine for three successive years. David sought the face of God and asked him the cause of the famine, which was a source of extreme suffering throughout the nation. God answered that the famine was a judgment against Israel for wrongs committed by King Saul against the Gibeonites who lived inside Israel's borders. Past generations of Israel had sworn to spare the life of the Gibeonites and their descendants, if they served Israel. Saul, in his zeal for a kind of racial cleansing had attempted to annihilate these people. When David asked them what he could do to make amends for the actions of the previous king, they requested the death of seven male descendants of Saul as justice for the crimes committed against them by Saul. David complied and God sent rain to break the famine.

When Joshua finally led the Hebrews across the Jordan after forty years of camping in the desert, God promised Joshua that he would give Israel every place they set their feet as they marched into the land that God had promised them. The first battle took Israel before the imposing stone walls of Jericho. Israel marched, trumpets sounded, and God gave them a miraculous victory. The city was dedicated to the Lord as first fruits and no one was to take any spoils from the city for personal use.

After celebrating God's powerful move on their part, Joshua determined that the next conquest should be the smaller less defended town of Ai. Scouting reports indicated that it should require only three thousand men to easily take this city while the others rested. However, as the Israelites struck at this insignificant city, they were routed and fled from the men of Ai. Joshua cried out to the Lord and accused God of failing to keep his promise to give them victory after victory. But God declared that Israel had sinned against him. In doing so, they had temporarily set aside the agreement of faith by their own actions.

When Joshua examined the camp to uncover Israel's sin, he discovered that one man, Achan, had taken clothing and gold for himself and hidden it in his tent. Because of his disobedience, many had fallen on the battlefield and God had removed his protection from a nation. The consequence of one man's sin was visited on his family, his friends, his tribe and his nation. Achan kept the plunder, but God said that Israel had sinned. After Achan's violation was discovered, he and his entire family were put to death for their sin. Only after that consequence, was God's protection over Israel restored.

Theologians call this the "principle of corporate solidarity" where the actions of one person are ascribed to those to whom he is connected—children, family, descendants, tribes or nations. The most well known expression of this principle is Adam's sin. As Adam sinned, the consequence or curse of death (separation from God and physical death) was visited upon him. "But you must not eat from the tree of the knowledge of good and evil, for when you eat of it you will surely die" (Gen. 2:17). The Apostle Paul tells us that because of one man's sin, death came to all men because all men are his descendants.

For many of us, this principle seems unjust. But God sets the standard, not man. God declares that this is a just principle and a righteous principle. It is also a necessary principle for the salvation of man. The flip side of this principle is that good things can also come to those connected to righteous men because of one man's righteousness. "For I, the LORD your God, am a jealous God, punishing the children for the sin of the fathers to the third and fourth generation of those who hate me, but showing love to a thousand generations of those who love me and keep my commandments" (Ex. 20:5-6). This principle is also the principle that allows Christ, as the Son of Man, to take on the sins of mankind that came to us through Adam and allows the righteousness of Christ to be ascribed to those who are his spiritual descendants by faith in him. As we were all in Adam when he sinned and all experienced the curse of sin by that connection, those of us who are in Christ experience the consequence of his righteousness, the blessing of eternal life.

> For if, by the trespass of the one man, death reigned through that one man, how much more will those who receive God's abundant provision of grace and of the gift of righteousness reign in life through the one man, Jesus Christ. (Rom. 5:17)

Not every negative experience is caused by a curse. Not every pain, struggle, or failure is caused by demonic oppression or attack. A curse is an unrelenting bent toward failure, disaster, sickness or oppression in the life of a family or individual, maintained by spiritual forces that have some legal standing or commission to maintain the curse. Frequently, bad things happen to good people simply because we live in a fallen world and have a fallen nature. Many bad things happen that are just part of life in a deranged universe. People get sick, they die, they are in tragic accidents, as a matter of life in a world un-submitted to God's perfect plan.

The ordinary litany of hardships on planet earth does constitute a general curse but not necessarily a curse that is attached to an individual or particular family. On the other hand, many people and families do seem to be stuck in unrelenting spirals of pain, failure, oppression and loss that do indicate the workings of a curse. The Bible lists a number of manifestations of curses and these are worth reviewing as we move ahead in this chapter.

Biblical Evidence of a Sin Curse

The following conditions are indicators that a curse may be operating in your life or in your family. If one or more of the following indicators repeatedly show up, generation after generation, there is possibly a *generational curse* at work. The key word is *repeatedly*.

1. **Poverty**

    Continual and repeated business failure and financial lack.

    Your basket and your kneading trough will be cursed ...You will sow much seed in the field but you will harvest little, because locusts will devour it. (Deut. 28:17, 18, 38)

2. **Infirmity**

    Consistent patterns of chronic, lingering, and incurable or undiagnosed diseases.

    The LORD will plague you with diseases until he has destroyed you from the land you are entering to possess. The LORD will strike you with wasting disease, with fever and inflammation, with scorching heat and drought, with blight and mildew, which will plague you until you perish. (Deut. 28:21- 22)

3. **Mental Illness**

    Patterns of mental illness, deep confusion, and emotional dysfunction.

    The LORD will send on you curses, confusion and rebuke in everything you put your hand to, until you are destroyed and come

to sudden ruin because of the evil you have done in forsaking him...
The LORD will afflict you with madness, blindness and confusion of
mind...The sights you see will drive you mad. (Deut. 28:20, 28, 34)

4. **Barrenness**
    Troubled pregnancy, difficulty conceiving, or multiple miscarriages.

The fruit of your womb will be cursed, and the crops of your land, and
the calves of your herds and the lambs of your flocks. (Deut. 28:18)

5. **Failure and Oppression**
    Constant patterns of failure, calamity, and disaster.

You will be cursed in the city and cursed in the country...You
will be cursed when you come in and cursed when you go out...
At midday you will grope about like a blind man in the dark. You
will be unsuccessful in everything you do; day after day you will
be oppressed and robbed, with no one to rescue you...The alien
who lives among you will rise above you higher and higher, but
you will sink lower and lower. He will lend to you, but you will
not lend to him. He will be the head, but you will be the tail.
(Deut. 28:16, 19, 29, 43-44)

6. **Misfortune**
    Disaster, disunity, and calamity in the home.

You will be pledged to be married to a woman, but another will
take her and ravish her. You will build a house, but you will not live
in it. You will plant a vineyard, but you will not even begin to enjoy
its fruit...Your sons and daughters will be given to another nation,
and you will wear out your eyes watching for them day after day,
powerless to a lift a hand... (Deut. 28:30, 32)

In general, a primary indicator of a generational curse is a pattern of
destructive behavior in a family and a pattern of consistent negative outcomes,
generation after generation. It is especially evident when believers are doing

the right things but destructive things continue to come their way. If we keep making bad decisions and getting bad results, it may simply be due to foolishness or a wrong response to woundedness on our part.

However, when events always seem to conspire against us, even when we have been sincerely trying to serve God, we may need to consider the possibility that a curse may be operating through family lines. If so, we should address that curse directly through the blood and authority of Jesus Christ. We will talk about that in detail at the end of this chapter.

Are We All Subject to Curses and Demonic Activity Associated With Them?

Solomon had something to say about curses. "Like a fluttering sparrow or a darting swallow, an undeserved curse does not come to rest" (Prov. 26:2). If there is no cause there will be no curse. If there is a cause, there may be a curse. The cause may be personal sin or it may be the "sins of the fathers" many generations ago. A great deal of this book is dedicated to teaching us how to live lives that are "undeserving" of curses and to apply the blood of Christ to any sin and consequent curse that may have come to us from our own sinful past or from our fathers. Before moving onto solutions, however, there is one other major source of curses in our lives beyond the sins to which God has attached curses. These are curses spoken by others or ourselves that give spiritual entities assignments in our lives.

Curses Spoken by Others Against Us

When many of us think about spoken curses, we reference old movies with witches dressed in black standing over boiling cauldrons, casting spells and declaring curses on their enemies or on the enemy of someone who has paid them for their sorceries. Perhaps, we think of satanic cults meeting in dark, candlelit basements or in remote forest glades under the stars, chanting curses against those that they hate. Hollywood has written these scenes in almost every possible way, from Disney's animated *Snow White* to any number of television series, depicting witches as being good wives and mothers fighting evil. We have seen this idea fictionalized so often that we tend to place the very concept of curses in the fictional realm. And yet, the idea of a spoken curse is very real.

Then the Israelites traveled to the plains of Moab and camped along the Jordan across from Jericho. Now Balak… Saw all that Israel had done to the Amorites, and Moab was terrified because there were so many people…So Balak…who was king of Moab at that time, sent messengers to summon Balaam son of Beor…Balak said: "A people has come out of Egypt; they cover the face of the land and have settled next to me. Now come and put a curse on these people, because they are too powerful for me. Perhaps then I will be able to defeat them and drive them out of the country. For I know that those you bless are blessed, and those you curse are cursed"… But God said to Balaam, "Do not go with them. You must not put a curse on those people, because they are blessed." (Num. 22:1-12)

Though we might dismiss the idea of spoken curses, God takes them seriously. Balak was a man who had a history with Balaam, at least as an observer. He said, "I know those you bless are blessed and those you curse are cursed." God commanded Balaam not to curse a people that he had blessed. Balaam had used sorcery in his past dealings. Sorcery is the art of influencing or commanding demonic spirits to do your bidding. In the context of a curse, sorcery would compel or invite demonic spirits to attack and oppress the person or group against whom the curse was spoken. Think of it as a prayer to Satan.

In prayer, we ask God to bless people we know. By faith, we believe that God will speak a word of authority over a situation and send angels to work in response to our prayer to bring about positive outcomes of protection, favor, blessing, healing, etc. In doing so, we sometimes ask for unfavorable outcomes for evil men. Those who serve Satan, pray to him, and ask him to send unclean spirits to work for unfavorable outcomes in the lives of an individual or group. Curses call on Satan to enter into lives and situations as well. If there is a cause, because of our sin or the sin of those we are connected to, then Satan has legal ground to act on the curse.

Words have power. In the first chapter of Genesis we discover that God exists and that his words have the power to create realities where nothing at all existed before. We are then told that God made man in his own image and gave him dominion (authority) over the earth. If God's declarations have the power to create and man is made in his image, then to a lesser degree, man's words and declarations have the power to create as well.

God creates directly, but man creates by setting spiritual forces in motion, which bring to pass those things that have been spoken…either blessing or cursing. Words have power and words may be spoken on our behalf or against us. When spoken on our behalf, they are blessings. When spoken against us, they may constitute a curse that settles into our lives, if there is a cause. This is particularly true when the one speaking the curse has spiritual authority over us such as a parent over a child, a husband over a wife, or a spiritual leader over a believer.

"The tongue has the power of life and death" (Prov. 18:21). We live in an age that surrounds us with noise, talking heads, and an overwhelming number of words. Because of that, we tend to dismiss the power of words and forget that in the spiritual realm, words are binding. In the natural realm, men hire lawyers and write contracts in ways that keep their words from binding them to implied commitments. But those games can't be played in the spiritual realm.

Jesus himself said, "You brood of vipers, how can you who are evil say anything good? For out of the overflow of the heart the mouth speaks. The good man brings good things out of the good stored up in him, and the evil man brings evil things out of the evil stored up in him. But I tell you that men will have to give account on the day of judgment for every careless word they have spoken. For by your words you will be acquitted, and by your words you will be condemned" (Matt. 12:34-37).

Curses do not have to be formalized declarations, chanted around glowing candles or a pentagram. Most of the time, they are not. They are simply words spoken in anger, bitterness, or frustration that still have the power to set forces in motion in the spiritual realm. Think of words spoken over children by angry or frustrated parents.

- *I wish you had never been born!*
- *You will never amount to anything!*
- *You're going to end up in prison just like your father!*
- *You're worthless. You're a loser and always will be.*
- *I hope you suffer like you have made me suffer!*
- *No one will ever want you!*

Although the parents who spoke these words in anger may never have meant to set forces in motion against their own children, they spoke them all the same. Like small print we failed to read on a contract, we may find ourselves reaping consequences for others we never intended. I'm not suggesting that every time we speak in frustration we establish a curse. But if we say things often enough or with enough intensity, some entity in the spiritual realm may take us up on our declaration. On numerous occasions in healing sessions, the Holy Spirit has revealed declarations made by parents in a moment of anger, fear, or frustration that established curses which operated in their child's life for years. These curses needed to be broken by the blood and authority of Jesus.

In a number of deliverance sessions, the Holy Spirit has prompted us to seek inner healing for an individual before deliverance. On several occasions, the Spirit has taken a woman back to a curse spoken over her by a parent while still in the womb. The mother, distressed by an unplanned and unwanted pregnancy, had spoken rejection or even death over the child in the womb, giving Satan legal access to bring torment and negative outcomes into the life of the child. When the wound had been healed by the truth of Jesus and the curse had been cancelled by his blood, then deliverance from spirits commissioned to maintain "the curse" could be accomplished.

There is power in words at many levels. Our words can shape a person's identity and self-image so that they consistently act in ways that confirm their beliefs about themselves for good or for bad. But there is also something prophetic about our words that call realities into being. The patriarchs of the Old Testament would gather their children around them as their time to die drew near and speak "the blessing" over them—especially over the firstborn. This blessing seems to have functioned as a prophetic word over the life of these adult children. It was part of their inheritance and was often seen as the most important part because it would surely come to pass. Jacob's mother so coveted the blessing for her son that she prompted him to deceive his father Isaac into believing that he was Esau. When Isaac had spoken the blessing over Jacob, Esau discovered the deception and cried out for his father to take back what he had spoken over Jacob. But Isaac could not take back what had already been declared and set into motion. Blessings declared over people impart life. But in the same way, curses declared over people may impart death—trouble, hindrance, negative outcomes, poor health, broken relationships, and so on.

When we begin to think about all the words we have ever spoken over others or had spoken over us, we can become very nervous. By God's grace, not every careless word spoken sets the spiritual realm in action, but some do. Often it is the bitterness, anger, or resentment that prompts the words that gives the enemy legal access to our lives. Curses, then, are indicated by patterns of failure, torment, bondage or disaster. The good news is that Jesus is greater than any weapon the enemy can form against us and his blood has the power to nullify any legal claim of the enemy — turning curses into blessings. "Because the one who is in you is greater than the one who is in the world" (1 John 4:4).

Self-Imposed Curses

In the previous section, we explored the potential source of a curse as the supernatural consequence ordained by God himself for certain un-repented sins. Secondly, we explored the potential for curses being directed at us by the words of others, spoken intentionally or unintentionally. Another source of curses is words spoken over us by ourselves. This section will explore the trap of self- imposed curses through our own words and silent vows, and how the blood of Christ sets us free from those curses as well.

> 'What shall I do, then, with Jesus who is called Christ?' Pilate asked. They all answered, 'Crucify him!' When Pilate saw that he was getting nowhere, but that instead an uproar was starting, he took water and washed his hands in front of the crowd. 'I am innocent of this man's blood,' he said, 'It is your responsibility!' All the people answered, 'Let his blood be on us and on our children!' Then he released Barabbas to them. But he had Jesus flogged, and handed him over to be crucified. (Matt. 27:22, 24-26)

In 70 A.D. the curse spoken by the leaders of Israel was fulfilled. Jerusalem was destroyed by Rome. In that destruction, thousands of Jews died, the temple was burned, the genealogies on which the priesthood was founded were destroyed, and the Jews were scattered all over the earth without a land to call their own for nearly 2000 years. The Jews who chose Barabbas over Jesus had declared a horrific curse over themselves that sent an entire nation into exile. This is an extreme example but how often do we speak negative, hurtful words and sentiments over ourselves?

Curses may be self-imposed when we speak hurtful words or judgments over ourselves.

Many of us struggle with our self-image, our sense of worth and our sense of competency. In Christ, all of our doubts about these issues are settled, but many believers live in agreement with Satan about who they are rather than in agreement with the Word of God. His Word declares that we are competent, righteous children in the household of God, men and women of destiny, royalty walking in the authority of the king, loved by God, citizens of heaven and more. Those things have been established by our position in Christ. Most of us, however, still choose to base our self-image on our condition rather than our position or on the opinion of other broken, wounded humans rather than on the declarations of God.

Most of us accumulate a library of negative messages about ourselves in our early years that emphasize our failings and shortcomings. The covert message behind all of these remarks is that we are unacceptable. Our self-image is drawn from the impressions we have about ourselves that were formed through the statements and actions of others. As we declare these judgmental statements over ourselves, our words may function as self-imposed curses, setting not only "self-fulfilling prophecies" into motion but spiritual forces as well that work to establish the things we have declared.

Just a few common declarations from hurting people are....

- I'll never amount to anything.
- Nothing will ever work out for me.
- I know I'll die young just like my father.
- Sooner or later, everyone will leave me.
- I'll never get out of debt.
- I would be better off dead.
- I'm just no good.
- I'm so stupid.
- I'm such a loser.
- No one could love me.
- My marriage will end in divorce.

Vows

Vows can also open the door to demonic activity in our lives. Vows are essentially declarations or promises we make to ourselves about what we are willing to do or not do in the future. Vows are like covenants we make with ourselves. We declare that we will never do something again or never be without something again. These vows are typically prompted by pain and are spoken as defensive measures against future pain.

The problem with a vow is that we yield that part of our lives to the lordship of the vow rather than to the lordship of Christ. It creates a pocket in our lives that even he won't touch. Vows fence off a part of our life, a wound or fear, that we will entrust to no one — not even Jesus. What we keep to ourselves, Jesus can't heal. Unhealed wounds are the very places where the enemy establishes strongholds.

Vows may be like contracts signed without reading the small print. They are still binding, though we were unaware of all the ramifications of what we swore to. What you have declared with your words may be done or enforced. Negative vows may function as self-imposed curses. If you meant the words in a figurative way, they may be applied literally by spiritual forces that use your words against you. Remember, the "tongue has the power of life and death" (Prov. 18:21).

Personal Reflection / Journaling:
- What evidence of curses do you see in your life or in your family history?
- Which parts of this chapter seemed to resonate with your spirit? What might that suggest to you?
- Are you aware of any judgments or vows you have declared over yourself consistently (or in response to some hurtful experience in your past)?
- Ask the Holy Spirit to reveal to you any curses, judgments or vows that have been standing in the way of your healing or freedom.

Memory Verse:
"The tongue has the power of life and death." (Prov. 18:21)

Chapter Eleven

BREAKING FREE

In my anguish I cried to the LORD, and he answered by setting me free.
(Ps. 118:5)

As we saw in the previous chapter, curses may be invited through our own sinful actions, by those of our ancestors, by others who have spoken condemning words over us, or by self-declared judgments and vows. Now the question becomes: If I am under a curse, can Jesus set me free? This chapter will answer that question with an emphatic "Yes" and show you the steps to break the power of a curse through Jesus Christ. Let's revisit Isaiah 61 and notice the emphasis I have added.

> The Spirit of the Sovereign LORD is on me, because the LORD has anointed me to preach good news to the poor. He has sent me to **bind up the brokenhearted**, to proclaim **freedom for the captives** and **release from darkness for the prisoners**, to proclaim the year of **the LORD's favor** and the day of vengeance of our God. (Isa. 61:1-2)

Jesus came to set people free who have been entangled by the nets of Satan, either by their own choices or by the destructive actions of others. The ransom has already been paid for past, present and future transgressions and curses. In the face of that, the enemy works tirelessly to weave lies into the fabric of God's truth so that those lies keep us from receiving all that God has for us.

Satan constantly reminds us of our sins, weaknesses, and failings. He whispers that God is beyond disappointed with us, there is a limit to his grace, and we have stepped over the line beyond his love or saving reach. The truth is that when we have been caught in Satan's nets, Jesus is not only willing to set us free the first time, but every time we cry out to him.

No matter what we have done or where we have been, whenever we turn our hearts to God and earnestly seek him, he is willing to deliver us from the power of the enemy. It is why Jesus came. Our escape has already been made sure in the Son. If you or your family live under a curse, the answer is in the cross of Christ.

Christ redeemed us from the curse of the law by becoming a curse for us... (Gal. 3:13)

Therefore, there is now no condemnation for those who are in Christ Jesus, because through Christ Jesus the law of the Spirit of life set me free from the law of sin and death. (Rom. 8:1-2)

Do you remember from earlier chapters, the great exchange that took place on the cross? Jesus took our place and gave us his. He became sin that we might become the righteousness of God. He became cursed so that we might be blessed. Jesus was willing to be taken prisoner so that we might be set free. Victory is assured but often we must engage in battle — with Jesus as our commander — to secure all the promises that are ours. As Israel crossed the Jordan and stepped onto a land that was theirs by promise, they still had to defeat enemies that inhabited the land. Many times, freedom in Christ is a process of liberation that may take a number of battles to fully root out the enemy and tear down his strongholds.

In the Pacific, after World War II, the Allies discovered numerous Japanese soldiers hiding on islands that had already been released to the Allies. These soldiers hid in caves, still fighting for an emperor who had already been defeated. The war was over and the outcome fully established, yet there were still pockets of resistance by a defeated enemy who would continue to harass and kill, if possible.

When Christ came to set us free, he knew that he was joining us in a lifelong process. The legal work has been done, the enemy has been found guilty, victory has been declared, but the enemy has to be rounded up and rooted out — sometimes by force. Jesus is willing to wield divine weapons with us time and again until the full work of liberation is completed. Sometimes in the battle we may lose ground because we did not stay close to our commander or obey his commands wholeheartedly. He is willing to stand with us again to retake ground if need be, or to take new ground that will be liberated for the first time. Breaking curses, casting out demons, crucifying the flesh, and healing deep wounds are all part of the process. But Jesus is able and willing to stand with us against the enemy and give us victory after victory when we trust him.

The Process of Cancelling a Curse

The process of nullifying or canceling a curse is a legal action through which you take away the cause and authority of the curse to continue to be in effect. It is the process of aligning ourselves with Christ and then nullifying the curse through the power of his blood and sacrifice.

The process includes...

Alignment
- A verbal declaration of the Lordship of Jesus and your allegiance to him.
- Humbling yourself before God through transparency and dependence on him.
- The confession of your sins and the sins of your fathers.
- Repentance and renouncement of those sins.
- Forgiving all those who have hurt or wronged you.

Declaration and the Exercise of Authority
- Breaking or nullifying the curse in the name of Jesus by his blood and by his authority.
- Expelling demons that may be attached to the curse.

Alignment

Alignment is about coming into agreement with Jesus in every area of your life...beliefs, thoughts, words, attitudes, and actions. It is about closing the gap between our condition and our position by making course adjustments as we go with Christ as our true north. The prophet Amos asked, "Can two walk together unless they are agreed?" (Amos 3:3) Who we agree with determines whom we walk with. If we agree with Satan, we walk with Satan. If we agree with Christ, we walk with Christ.

Alignment is coming into agreement with Jesus and renouncing any former agreements with Satan. Verbal declarations are important. You can think something in your mind or carry an intent in your heart, but until you declare it verbally or in writing (with your signature), it is not binding. A good way to begin the alignment process is to verbally declare your allegiance to Jesus — that you stand with him — and verbally renounce the works of Satan.

Humbling yourself before God is also essential. At the crux of Satan's rebellion and his temptation of Adam and Eve was the notion of self-sufficiency. When we believe that we can handle life in our own strength, we are declaring that God is incidental. When we maintain that attitude, we are in agreement with Satan. James encourages us when he says, "Resist the devil and he will flee from you" (James 4:7). Note that the verse immediately preceding it says, "Submit yourselves, then, to God." Submitting to the Lord is the key to resisting the devil. As we submit to God or humble ourselves before him, we acknowledge his Lordship and our need for his covering. We then line up under his authority so his power is available to us. Satan has no fear of man when he stands alone or resists alone. He only flees when the power and authority of Christ is present to back up our resistance.

Next in aligning ourselves with Christ is the confession and repentance of sin. This simply means that we agree with God about sin and his standards. Remember, he promises to forgive our sins and cleanse us from unrighteousness when we confess our sins. It is understood that our confession comes out of a penitent heart and godly sorrow.

Next, however, is the confession of "the sins of our fathers." As Daniel was interceding with God on behalf of the Hebrew people, he prayed: "Lord, you are righteous, but this day we are covered with shame—the men of Judah and people of Jerusalem and all Israel, both near and far, in all the countries where you have scattered us because of our unfaithfulness to you. O Lord, we and our kings, our princes and our fathers are covered with shame because we have sinned against you" (Dan. 9:7-8).

Notice that Daniel confessed his own sin, the sin of the nation's leaders, and the sins of the fathers. I believe this is in response to the declaration of

God that the sins of the fathers will be visited on the children to the third and fourth generations. Curses are attached to un-repented and unconfessed sin. Daniel, therefore, stood in proxy for the fathers and confessed sin in their stead, coming into agreement with God about those actions.

Nehemiah followed suit with Daniel in his prayer for Jerusalem. "In all that has happened to us, you have been just; you have acted faithfully, while we did wrong. Our kings, our leaders, our priests and our fathers did not follow your law; they did not pay attention to your commands or the warnings you gave them" (Neh. 9:33-34). Nehemiah confessed the sinfulness of all those in authority; from kings to lesser leaders, to spiritual leaders, and then fathers.

Generational curses attached to the sins of fathers give Satan legal ground to enforce the curses attached to those sins. Confession of these past sins removes Satan's legal ground to harass and oppress the children of those who sinned. Simply declaring their sins is not sufficient, however. God's forgiveness comes to those whose hearts are turned toward him, who are sincerely sorrowful for their sins and the failings of their fathers. Such hearts move God to deliver them from the power of the enemy.

> When all these blessings and curses I have set before you come upon you and you take them to heart wherever the LORD your God disperses you among the nations, and when you and your children return to the LORD your God and obey him with all your heart and with all your soul according to everything I command you today, then the LORD your God will restore your fortunes and have compassion on you and gather you again from all the nations where he scattered you. (Deut. 30:1-3).

A final and sometimes more difficult aspect of aligning ourselves with God is extending forgiveness to those who have wronged us, We talked about this extensively earlier in this book, so there is no need to go over that ground again, other than to restate the requirement. All unforgiven sin gives Satan legal access to us. God says that only when we forgive others will he forgive us. Our refusal to forgive others is simply evidence that our hearts are not aligned with God's heart, and that is Satan's open door.

Declarations

Having aligned ourselves with Christ, then his power and authority can flow through us. Having removed Satan's legal ground to maintain a curse in our lives, we can then declare with authority that the curse is no longer binding and has been nullified by the blood and sacrifice of Christ. "Christ redeemed us from the curse of the law by becoming a curse for us, for it is written: 'Cursed is everyone who is hung on a tree.' he redeemed us in order that the blessing given to Abraham might come to the Gentiles through Christ Jesus, so that by faith we might receive the promise of the Spirit" (Gal. 3:13-14).

We can declare with authority that the curse is no longer in effect because Christ himself took on the curse of the law through his death on the cross. As we come into agreement with him, then we have full access to the blessings he purchased for us through his death. Having dealt with the curse through the blood of Christ, any demonic assignments that were attached to the curse can be cancelled and those unclean spirits can be driven out also by the authority of Jesus Christ.

The following are suggested prayers for the breaking of curses and vows. I encourage you to familiarize yourself with these prayers so that you will be able to speak them with understanding and agreement when you go through the process of breaking curses.

Prayer and Declarations for Breaking Curses...

Lord Jesus Christ, I believe that you are the Son of God and the only way to the Father — that you died on the cross for my sins and rose again that I might be forgiven and receive eternal life. I renounce all pride, self-righteousness and self-sufficiency and declare my total dependence on you for life, righteousness and freedom. I have no claim on your mercy except your unfailing love for me that moved you to die on the cross in my place.

I confess to you all my sins and the sins of my fathers, known and unknown, and hold nothing back. I especially confess (any and all persistent sin in your life or known sins of your ancestors). I renounce and repent of these sins and every work of Satan. I turn away from them and I turn to you, Lord, for mercy and forgiveness based on your shed blood on the cross.

By a decision of my will, I freely forgive all who have ever harmed or wronged me. I surrender all anger, bitterness, resentment and revenge to the cross. Because you paid a debt I could not pay, I no longer require any payment for the wrongs done to me. I release all judgment of these matters to you, Jesus, the righteous judge. Specifically, in the name of Jesus I forgive (people you have not forgiven).

Lord, I thank you that on the cross you became a curse for me, that I might be redeemed from every curse and inherit God's blessings. On the basis of your death, your shed blood, your burial, and your resurrection, I now renounce every curse or judgment ever established against me, based on sin or spoken words. Now by the blood, the name, and the promises of Jesus Christ, I cancel every curse or judgment, making them null and void. By the sword of the Spirit, I sever myself from their effects.

Also, by the blood, the authority, and the name of Jesus, I cancel any demonic assignments associated with those curses. In his name, I take authority over any and every unclean spirit that has been assigned to the curse. I bind you and cast you out now. I command you to leave immediately and to never return. I command this in the sovereign name of Jesus Christ who has all authority in heaven and on earth.

Jesus, thank you for becoming a curse, that I might be blessed. I ask you now, on the basis of your blood, power and authority, to establish these things that I have declared in your name and according to your will. Set me and my family free that we might now receive the blessings you have purchased for us with your blood.

In Jesus' name...Amen.

Prayer for Releasing Vows...

In the name of Jesus, I renounce any and all vows that I knowingly or unknowingly made in my past that were not aligned with God's will and purposes. I repent of giving lordship to those vows and for refusing to submit those parts of my life to Jesus. I now declare that Jesus is the only Lord of my life and I willingly submit every part of my life to him. By the blood of Christ, I cancel these vows; I declare them null, void and without influence in my life. By the sword of the Spirit, I sever myself from the effects of these vows. Lord Jesus, by your authority, I ask you to seal off any entry points into my life by which Satan gained access to me and my family because of these past vows.

In addition, by the blood and the name of Jesus, I cancel any demonic assignments associated with those vows. In his name I take authority over any and every unclean spirit that has been assigned to the vow and I sever any hold they ever had on me. In the name of Jesus, by his blood and authority, I bind you and cast you out now. In Jesus' name, I command you to leave me immediately and never return.

You have no place in me. Your legal claims have been taken away and you have no right to be present in my life, from this moment forward. Jesus became sin for me that I might be the righteousness of God. He became a curse for me so that I might be set free from any curse. The Word of God declares that since the Son has set me free, I am free indeed. You are defeated and cast down. I pull down every stronghold by the mighty name and the authority of Jesus Christ, by the power of his resurrection and the power of the cross. I nullify and cast out every lie sown by the enemy. I command you to leave immediately and to never return. I command this in the sovereign name of Jesus Christ, who has all authority in heaven and on earth.

Jesus, your Word declares that you have all authority in heaven and earth and that you have a name that is above every name in this age and the age to come. When you walked this earth, you demonstrated your power over the enemy and cast out every kind of demon. You demonstrated your victory over Satan by your resurrection from the grave. Hell could not hold you. Satan, you and all your demons are defeated and your power is broken this day in my life.

The old is past and the new has come. Jesus, thank you for dying that I might live. Thank you for becoming a curse that I might be blessed. Thank you for defeating the enemy and for breaking his power in my life that I might be set free. Strengthen me now to walk in this freedom and to be pleasing to you in every way...Amen.

Soul Ties

There is one area left to discuss that is related to bondage in the spiritual realm. "Soul ties" is not a biblical term, nor is it well defined in Scripture though it is hinted at. Those who have long years of experience in spiritual warfare and the use of divine weapons seem to agree that these "ties" exist.

There are entire books that discuss the concept, but I will attempt to lay out briefly the core issues related to this concept.

The concept of *soul ties* is that our connection with people in the physical realm may also establish binding connections in the spiritual realm as with marriage. In the Gospel of Matthew, Jesus discusses marriage and divorce. He clearly says that what has been established in the physical realm has also been established and is binding in the spiritual realm. God has joined two people together and he oversees the covenant rather than the state or the courts of men.

> Haven't you read," he replied, "that at the beginning the Creator 'made them male and female,' and said, 'For this reason a man will leave his father and mother and be united to his wife, and the two will become one flesh'? So they are no longer two, but one. Therefore what God has joined together, let man not separate. (Matt. 19:4-6)

In 2 Corinthians, Paul tells us that there are relationships that yoke us, tie us, or commit us to other people. It is the idea that something binding and influential exists in the relationship. It may be a relationship of simple influence or it may be formalized through a written or verbal covenant or contract. Clearly, these "yoked" relationships create concerns that extend into the spiritual realm and, at the least, seem offensive to God. They seem to bring us into alignment with Satan in some way that hinders the flow of God's grace and Spirit in our lives.

> Do not be yoked together with unbelievers. For what do righteousness and wickedness have in common? Or what fellowship can light have with darkness? What harmony is there between Christ and Belial? What does a believer have in common with an unbeliever? What agreement is there between the temple of God and idols? (2 Cor. 6:14-16)

In addition to formal covenants, Scripture suggests that there is something spiritually binding about sexual unions. It is a union that is to be reserved for marriage only. Paul speaks about sexual union outside the marriage bond in his second letter to the Corinthian church, where sexual immorality was part of the very fiber of the city. This is a Scripture that is hard to understand, but it uses the language of union and marriage and attaches that language to sexual relationships outside of marriage.

> The body is not meant for sexual immorality...Do you not know that your bodies are members of Christ himself? Shall I then take the members of Christ and unite them with a prostitute? Never! Do you not know that he who unites himself with a prostitute is one with her in body? For it is said, "The two will become one flesh." But he who unites himself with the Lord is one with him in spirit. Flee from sexual immorality. All other sins a man commits are outside his body, but he who sins sexually sins against his own body. (1 Cor. 6:13-18)

Over the years, one of the most consistent counseling issues I have seen with couples who had a sexual history with others before they married, is the continuing influence of these past relationships — especially in the marriage bed. On several occasions I have met with one of the spouses who came alone to confess the struggle. Often the past sexual relationships were experienced before they came to Christ. Often in this transitional phase of their lives, they have come to the Lord with a sincere heart and have desired holiness and purity in their marriage that they have never known before.

But what they come to confess is their inability to forget their past sexual experiences. Often, in their minds they are once again in bed with an old boyfriend or girlfriend rather than the spouse they love. They feel defiled by the experience as well as being plagued by feelings of guilt and shame. It is as if the sexual union established a "spiritual yoke" that still influences them and calls them back to their past. They seem unable to fully embrace their new marriage in the Lord because they feel "tied" to these past relationships. Taking these men and women through a process of repentance and breaking these ties has made an immediate difference for many of these couples.

The idea of *soul ties,* then, is that at a spiritual level we have entered into implied or spoken covenants that keep us bound to people from our past so that we cannot move into our future or give ourselves fully to God or a spouse. I find also that individuals seem to be tied to hurtful people from their past — controlling or abusive parents or other authority figures in their lives. The yoking here may have been against a person's will but the exercise of spiritual authority in the past by these hurtful individuals may still tie us to them.

Indicators of Soul Ties

- We may continue to feel drawn to our past so that we cannot emotionally or psychologically move into our future.
- We may fantasize about past relationships or sexual sin against our will.
- We may feel as if we can't fully give ourselves to a godly relationship or marriage because of past sexual unions.
- We may feel that people from our past still have a negative, controlling influence in our lives even though we rarely or never see them.
- We struggle with obsessive memories or thoughts about past relationships.
- Although we have forgiven those who have wounded us in the past, we cannot seem to receive healing, nor escape the painful memories.

How to Break Soul Ties

As with all healing and freedom, there is a process.

- Acknowledge any past sexual sin or sinful relationships (including those that were against your will — incest, molestation, rape, etc.) and lift these up to the Lord for healing and forgiveness.
- Acknowledge covenants (promises, commitments) that you made that you had no right to make or did not intend to keep.
- Acknowledge covenants and promises made to unbelievers that caused you to compromise your faith in any way.
- Repent of sins, ungodly covenants, and lies that you spoke to others to manipulate them for your own gratification.
- Ask God to forgive you and release you from your past on the basis of the blood of Christ shed for your sins.
- Ask God, by the blood of Christ, to break any and all bonds that you may have with hurtful people or people with whom you have sinned or made ungodly covenants in the past.
- Recommit your relationships to Jesus and submit to his standards.
- Pray for holiness and wisdom in your current and future relationships.
- Have others pray over you. (James 5:16)
- Ask God to show you if there is anything you must do in the natural realm to be released from ungodly relationships that have also been established in the spiritual realm. Seek confirmation through godly

counsel and prayer before taking action on what you believe God has shown you.

Before praying, ask yourself which past relationships still haunt your memories, still invade your thoughts, draw you back, or keep you from moving ahead. Which past relationships seem to have impacted your life in a negative, sinful or hurtful way? Who are the people that represent those relationships to you?

- List the people that come to mind.
- List the sin(s) that you participated in willingly.
- List the sin(s) in which you were forced to participate.
- List the hurtful behaviors that were imposed on you.
- Pray the following prayer or one like it over each of those relationships.

Prayer for Breaking Soul Ties...

Heavenly Father, I come to you in the name of Jesus, made righteous by his blood. I thank you that you are Lord over my past, present, and future. I thank you that you have given all authority in heaven and on earth to my Lord and High Priest, Jesus Christ. In the name of Jesus, I confess and renounce all past sins in which I have been willingly or unwillingly involved.

In particular, I renounce the sins of _____

_____

In the name and by the blood of your Son, Jesus Christ, I ask your forgiveness for the sins I willingly participated in and I ask for cleansing from the sins that I participated in unwillingly. I also confess ungodly covenants and relationships in my past I established, contrary to your will, intentionally and unintentionally. I renounce those covenants and renounce all my past sinful and destructive relationships that were not submitted to you.

Now, in the name of Jesus, by his blood and by his authority, I ask you to cancel all covenants from my past that were not godly covenants. I ask you to sever, by the sword of the Spirit, all ties that may have been established between me and (name those who still influence your thoughts, feelings or decisions in negative ways):

_____

In Jesus' name, I now place these relationships under the Lordship of Jesus and under his blood and declare my complete freedom in him. Jesus, thank you for forgiving my past and for setting me free. May I walk only in your will in my relationships in all my days to come.

It is in your name I pray...Amen.

Personal Reflection / Journaling:

- What has God shown you concerning curses that have been operating in your life or in your family line?
- What has he spoken to you about those curses? Write down any insight, revelation, or direction concerning those curses?
- What curses or inner vows do you believe you recognized as you went through the material in this chapter? Have you already prayed for those to be broken? If not, what keeps you from doing so?
- Ask Jesus if there is anything else that needs to be dealt with in the area of curses.
- If you prayed for soul ties to be broken, do you sense that God has released you from any past relationships so that you can now move ahead in freedom?
- Is there anything you believe he has asked you to do in the natural before any of those ties can be severed? Write down what that may be and share this with a spiritual mentor before acting on it.

Suggested Prayer

Lord, I need you. I need your grace and power in my life to set me free. I ask for the Spirit of wisdom and revelation so that I might know you better. I also pray that the eyes of my heart might be enlightened by your Spirit so that I may fully know the hope that I have in you and the riches that I have in Christ and the power that is available through you for me. Lord, increase my faith and my trust and fill me with a greater and greater measure of your Spirit, that I might live for you and experience all that you have for me. In Jesus' name I pray...Amen.

Memory Verse:

"Being confident of this, that he who began a good work in you will carry it on to completion until the day of Christ Jesus." (Phil. 1:6)

TRANSITIONAL NOTE

You have now finished the overview and theology of healing and freedom. If you are ready to trust Jesus, take him at his word, and act on his promises then this next section is for you. It is a compilation of every prayer and declaration set out in the Part One of this book, plus some additional prayers and declarations so that you can move through the process without looking back and forth in the text.

Pray about moving through the process. Ask Jesus when to begin, if your heart is in the right place and if there is someone appointed by Jesus to help walk you through the process or parts of the process. All you really need is Jesus, but Jesus often likes to include others. All of this has been purchased for you by the blood of Jesus. His intent is to set you free so that you can give love and receive loved as he intended.

Jesus replied: " 'Love the Lord your God with all your heart and with all your soul and with all your mind.' This is the first and greatest commandment. And the second is like it: 'Love your neighbor as yourself.' All the Law and the Prophets hang on these two commandments" (Mt.22:37-40).

Blessings as you find your freedom and healing in the Lord!

THE PROCESS
OF FREEDOM

COMING INTO ALIGNMENT

The following pages put together a process for helping people find freedom in Jesus Christ. In some ways, it is a summary of everything we have talked about in this book without the commentary. It is a summary of...

- All the action steps that will bring you into agreement or alignment with Christ.
- All the steps to nullify Satan's authority to maintain strongholds in your life.
- All the steps for taking authority over the demonic forces that have kept you from experiencing a full relationship with Jesus.

Before going further, however, I want to insert a word of warning and encouragement, beginning with the words of Jesus.

When an evil spirit comes out of a man, it goes through arid places seeking rest and does not find it. Then it says, 'I will return to the house I left.' When it arrives, it finds the house swept clean and put in order. Then it goes and takes seven other spirits more wicked than itself, and they go in and live there. And the final condition of that man is worse than the first. (Luke 11:24-26)

Jesus spoke of a man who had been delivered from a wicked spirit. Maybe it was a tormenting spirit, a spirit of bondage to some sin, or a spirit that affected the man's health. We don't know. But what is apparent is that the man sought the power of God in his life only for personal benefit and not out of a desire for a deeper relationship with God. When the man found freedom and his house was put in order, a vacancy was created. He had an available room but had not decided to whom he would give the room.

Jesus spoke the following words to the church of Laodicea in his letters to the seven churches of Asia "Here I am! I stand at the door and knock. If anyone hears my voice and opens the door, I will come in and eat with him, and he with me" (Rev. 3:20). Jesus desires to enter our hearts — to have an intimate and lasting relationship with us. The enemy desires to hinder that relationship. Our goals for healing and freedom should not merely be for personal benefit, although that will certainly occur. Our primary goal must be to know and experience more of Jesus. If the man whose house was put in order had immediately invited Jesus in as master of the house, there would have been no vacancy. But a spiritual vacuum was created, the room was left available, and the enemy returned to that empty place more powerfully than before.

John Bevere, in his book A *Heart Ablaze,*[1] makes a strong point that as believers in the 21st Century, many of us seek God only in the things that satisfy our flesh…our personal version of the "prosperity gospel." We depart from him when he calls us to the things we don't truly desire, while still calling him Lord. God's grace is not intended as a *cover-up* for the sinful desires we pursue, but rather is the power to overcome the flesh and live holy lives before God.

If you seek freedom only to feel better, to break the curse of poverty, or even to save your marriage while not truly desiring an intimate relationship with God, you may be left with an empty house vulnerable to the return of the enemy. Jesus certainly wants to free you and bless you. As I have said, that is why he came, but he first wants our hearts and an intimate relationship with us.

When the bride marries the bridegroom, the motive should be love not money. If she marries only for money or for personal benefit, that will soon become obvious and the marriage will be a sham. If she marries for love, however, and love compels her to serve her husband with joy…then all that he has will also be gladly given to her. When we seek Christ with all of our hearts and want to know him fully, then not only will we receive freedom but much more. If we seek this freedom for only selfish motives, we place ourselves in jeopardy.

So as freedom comes, pursue Christ and the things of Christ with all your heart. Be radical. Give the enemy no place in your life...not even an inch. Pursue the biblical standards of holiness rather than our society's standards or even American church standards that have often shifted with the culture. Determine to seek God's favor and not the favor of man. Determine not to fit in with the world but to be fully pleasing to God. Guard your heart, your eyes and your thoughts. Surrender everything to Jesus Christ. Seek first the Kingdom of God and his righteousness and then God will provide everything else you need for joy, peace and significance. Now...on to finding freedom.

Preparing with Prayer

As you approach the following exercises that lead to freedom, I encourage you to set aside time for prayer each day for several days asking the Lord to show you anything that is still standing in the way of your relationship with him and your freedom in Christ. Fasting for a period of time would also be of special benefit.

Personal Assessment

When we speak of opening our hearts to Christ, we often think in terms of being open to receive his love. That is certainly a very important part of the process, but it is also important to open our hearts to Christ for inspection and cleansing. Jesus not only wants to sit in the neat, clean living room of our hearts that we keep tidy for visitors, but he also wants to visit the back rooms full of clutter and the closet doors with locks on them. He even wants to look under the beds. Only then can he touch and heal. Only then can he truly set us free. Be willing to open every door and let him be Lord over every part of your heart. Then you will be free.

Prayerfully go back over any areas in your life that may still not be submitted to Jesus. Take a thorough inventory. If God calls it sin, you call it sin. Be ruthless. Do not minimize, justify or rationalize. Call it sin and take personal responsibility for it. Here is a beginning outline to help you evaluate this part of your life.

1. Have you, with a sincere heart, asked Jesus to be your Lord and Savior on the basis of your personal faith and his sacrificial death on your behalf?

2. If Jesus has been your savior, have you truly made him Lord over every aspect of your life? Are there any areas of your life you have reserved for the flesh and not surrendered to Jesus? Which areas?

3. Are any works of the flesh or sinful nature evident in your life? List any areas you need to acknowledge, confess, and repent of. Ask God to show you areas that are hidden from you. Ask people who are close to you what they see in your life.

> So I say, live by the Spirit, and you will not gratify the desires of the sinful nature. For the sinful nature desires what is contrary to the Spirit, and the Spirit what is contrary to the sinful nature. They are in conflict with each other, so that you do not do what you want. But if you are led by the Spirit, you are not under law. The acts of the sinful nature are obvious... (Gal. 5:16-19, see also verses 20-21)

- Sexual immorality (of any kind) including lust, sexual fantasies, pornography, any sexual involvement outside of marriage, etc.

- Impurity — participating in things offensive to God, touching spiritually or morally "unclean" things, having improper motives, being double-minded about your love for Jesus and love for the world, etc.

- Debauchery — unbridled lust, insolence, shamelessness, excess, lack of restraint in sexual areas, food, spending, language, partying, etc.

- Idolatry — desiring anything or anyone more than God. Seeking a source other than God for your identity, security or significance. Putting anything else above your commitment to Jesus, making him second place to a relationship, career, recreational activity, money, etc.

- Witchcraft — occult involvement, magical arts, use of mind-altering drugs for spiritual experiences, participating in false religions, horoscopes, tarot cards, etc. (We will discuss this area more fully later in this chapter.)

- Hatred — despising others in your heart, desiring hurt for another, desire for revenge.

- Discord — being the cause of strife or division, stirring up trouble, manipulating others so that they are at odds with one another. This usually includes gossip and slander.

- Jealousy — envy, desiring what others have, while resenting those who have it.

- Fits of rage — uncontrolled anger or resentment, fits of temper, punishing behaviors toward others.

- Selfish ambition — seeking power and status for personal gain or glorification, self-absorption, self-promotion, egocentrism, "it's all about me." Often associated with manipulation and controlling behaviors. Always places personal needs above the needs of others.

- Dissensions — creating division and promoting factions. Actions that promote disunity in families, groups, business places, among friends or in the church.

- Factions — creating groups, sects, religious parties separate from the Body of Christ. Drawing believers away from established leadership by personal teachings and a desire to "be in charge."

- Envy — perhaps a subtle form of jealousy that manifests more as resentment and judgment than as overt anger.

- Drunkenness — intoxication, drinking to the extent that judgment and restraint are compromised.

- Orgies — unrestrained partying, drinking parties, carousing.

- And the like — Anything else that God has shown you that is contrary to his will for you.

An additional inventory might also include taking a look at the fruit of the Spirit and seeing if you have any "fruit" of a different spirit that is often evident in your life. Read this passage and see if you manifest behaviors or attitudes that are opposite or contrary to his fruit.

"But the fruit of the Spirit is love, joy, peace, patience, kindness, goodness, faithfulness, gentleness and self-control. Against such things there is no law." (Gal. 5:22-23)

Write down any areas you see that are contrary to the fruit of the Spirit and add them to your list for confession and repentance. Consider the destructive aspects of these behaviors or attitudes in your life and the lives you touch, as well as their offensive nature to God.

4. In regard to unforgiveness, are there any individuals for whom you still hold grudges, resentment, or anger that you have not yet released to God? Just because you have locked them away in old memories does not mean you have forgiven them. Ask the Spirit to bring to mind any old hurts and wounds, and the individuals that inflicted those on you. You may need to search your memory for childhood events at school or on the playground. Think of teachers who were unfair, or of old boyfriends or girlfriends who hurt you. These seem so long ago that you may want to discount them, but the enemy may still use them for legal grounds to afflict you.

Write down any individuals against whom you have carried hatred or resentment and for whom you have not *formally* declared forgiveness.

5. Areas of guilt, shame, and fear you have not yet opened up to Jesus.

Sometimes, these areas are more difficult to deal with than sin because there is so much hurt and fear of experiencing again the hurt associated with them. *Guilt* is the feeling that I have done something wrong that still needs to be punished or that remains unforgiven. *Shame* is the feeling that there is something wrong with me that makes me forever unacceptable to God or others.

List any past experiences that produced shame, guilt, fear, feelings of unworthiness, rejection, etc. that you have hidden away from Christ. Ask his Spirit to bring to mind any areas that need to be visited by Jesus for your healing. Listen quietly after praying and pay attention over the next day or two to old memories that surface in your mind. Write those down and choose to submit those memories to his healing touch. These experiences are not hidden away from Christ, only from you. These "skeletons in the closet" need to be released to him and disposed of by his grace.

6. Addictions which are forms of bondage that take many shapes.

Addictions are not just chemical or sexual dependencies. An addiction is anything other than God that we go to consistently for comfort, security, feelings of significance, worth, or to numb emotional pain. Addictions may include video games, social networks, food, shopping, sex, vocations, recreational pursuits, romance, approval, or adrenalin. Take an inventory of your life. Are there any things that call you, seduce you and consistently keep you from what God would want for you? If so, acknowledge them and list them here for confession, prayer and, perhaps, deliverance later.

7. Past sinful or hurtful relationships you have not yet acknowledged.

This falls in the area of soul ties and unconfessed sin. Both of these make you vulnerable to the enemy. Sometimes we simply don't want to talk about our past because of pain or shame. But those things from our past that have impacted us negatively need to be brought into the light to be cleansed of their toxic properties. Our past needs to be purified by letting Christ shine his light on past relationships. They need to be healed, forgiven and cleansed by the Good Shepherd. If there are any that you have not yet laid before the Lord, list those and trust him to deal with your past with love and kindness for he is "gentle and humble in heart, and you will find rest for your souls" (Matt. 11:29).

8. Past occult experiences or involvements you have not renounced.

Occult practices create a wide open door that gives the enemy full permission to enter. All occult activity is an open door to the spiritual realm, inviting unclean spirits to enter, masquerading as angels of light. Jesus isn't the only one who stands at the door and knocks. Many of us think of satanic cults, animal sacrifices, and witches reading incantations from ancient books as occult involvement or witchcraft. But many other things are related.

Any activities that look to sources in the spirit realm other than God for answers to life's problems are occult. Spirits behind occult activities are not the Holy Spirit. They are demonic spirits who seek to deceive and destroy. Witchcraft, sorcery, divination, and channeling (mediums) were capital crimes in the Old Testament because these activities opened the door to the destructive activities of the enemy.

America is enthralled with these activities today. I have personally known a number of conservative, white-collar Americans who have participated in witches covens, satanic rituals or Wicca. For most, it was a season of curiosity or exploration of spiritual realities. As teens, many of us participated in séances, used Ouija boards, messed around with tarot cards, or visited a fortune-teller at a carnival, etc. thinking it was just fun and games. Some of us have participated in "service organizations" that employed secret initiation rituals, oaths and vows for membership or, at least, for higher levels of leadership in the organization. These may have seemed like harmless traditions (like secret handshakes of a college fraternity), but many of these have occult roots and our words are taken seriously in the spiritual realm, even if we spoke them in the spirit of fun and camaraderie.

Make a list of any possible occult experiences you have participated in at one time or another. You may want to review the indicators listed under the spirit of divination (Prayers and Declarations section) to help you with this inventory. Certainly, if you have been involved in any occult experiences in an ongoing way or know that your parents, grandparents or great grandparents were, this is certainly an open door you'll want to close through confession, repentance and deliverance.

There are certain cultures that are very prone to the use of "white" magic as means of healing and protection. Many believers who would never engage in such things had favorite grandmothers who often dabbled in the arts of white magic in their small towns or neighborhoods. Demons may attach as family spirits and continue to harass and deceive from generation to generation. Ask the Lord to show you anything in this area that needs to be submitted to the blood of Christ so that nothing hinders your freedom in Christ. Also be aware of "Christian" movements that hold unbiblical views of Jesus and that look to sources of authority or leaders that are not fully aligned with God's Word.

9. Contemporary idolatry you have not recognized and renounced.

Many of us in America have designated idols in our homes to which we pray or sacrifice. However, idolatry, like witchcraft, is the act of seeking security, direction, power, protection, provision or significance from a source other than God. It takes the form of devotion and we give ourselves and our resources to a false God believing that this false God will provide what we need for health and happiness. In the modern world, we make idols of careers, relationships, recreational pursuits, celebrities, fame, sex, addictions — you name it. We devote ourselves to these things, believing that somehow they will be the source of what we need for the abundant life. Satan often fuels these pursuits as ways to draw us away from God. Ask God to show you the "God substitutes" in your life. To what things have you given time, energy, emotion, financial resources, and devotion that have been a higher priority in your life than your relationship with God?

10. Receiving God's forgiveness.

One final area you may want to consider is the issue of receiving God's forgiveness or, in a sense, forgiving yourself for past sins and transgressions that may still stir feelings of guilt or shame in you. I have often sat across from godly Christians who confess, "I know I'm forgiven, but I don't feel forgiven." They have gone to God numerous times seeking absolution for the same past sin. They have confessed it, cried over it, and beat themselves up for it innumerable times. For some, it was a past affair, for others an abortion. For some it was a season of child abuse, a homosexual episode, or an unexplained criminal act that was never discovered or prosecuted. They know that they have done what God requires for forgiveness but they have not yet been able to truly receive it in their hearts. As a result, they always feel a bottleneck in their joy, thanksgiving and in their relationship with God. I don't have a quick solution for this problem of the soul but I have some observations that may lead to some helpful steps.

First of all, we sometimes fail to receive God's grace in forgiveness because being forgiven does not match our view of ourselves. We still relate to ourselves on the basis of our condition rather than our position. In this area, we must walk by faith and not by sight. We must learn to say about ourselves what God says about us by confessing our identity in Christ at every opportunity.

Secondly, many people believe they are forgiven on the basis of the depth of their sorrow and self-loathing rather than on the cross of Christ. It seems they believe that when they have punished themselves long enough and severely enough to demonstrate a particular depth of sorrow for a particular sin, God will see their sincerity from above and finally forgive them. Yet to do so is to declare that Christ's blood and God's grace are insufficient. We cannot pay for sin that has already been fully paid for. Declare your full forgiveness in Christ at every opportunity.

When receiving God's forgiveness we need to understand his heart. God does not live in the past; he lives in the future and calls the things that are not as though they already are. His mercies are new every morning. When we come to God in genuine repentance, he is quick to remove our sins as far as the east is from the west and to blot them out totally with an eraser soaked in the blood of his Son. This is not about "feeling forgiven" as much as it is about declaring our forgiveness in the face of contrary emotions. The Word of God- not our emotions- confirms our total forgiveness in Christ.

If you struggle with this, ask the Holy Spirit to do a work in your heart. Consistently say what God says about these things, and ask several faithful Christian intercessors to pray for you about this matter. Ask Jesus to speak to you personally about your past, your forgiveness and his desires for you. In addition, you may find that spirits of rejection, accusation and condemnation have been preventing you from making progress in this area. Deliverance in the name of Jesus will also allow you to move forward in receiving God's great gift.

11. Other

Write down anything else you still need to submit to Jesus or have others pray about with you.

End Notes:

1. John Bevere, *A Heart Ablaze* (Thomas Nelson Publishers, 1999)

Release from
Your Past

"So if the Son sets you free, you will be free indeed." (John 8:36)

This is a time for freedom. If you are in Christ, then Satan has no power over you except the power you give him. This is the time in which, by the blood and the authority of Jesus Christ, you may remove all legal access that Satan may have had to you and your family. This is the time when the power of sin can be broken in your life. Jesus came to set you free. By his death and his resurrection, he has defeated darkness and has been given all authority in heaven and on earth. He has been given a name that is above every name — that at his name, every knee shall bow and every tongue confess that Jesus is Lord. It is by his blood and his authority that you will experience healing and freedom.

The declarations and exercises in the remainder of this book are designed to align you with Christ and to take away all legal ground from the enemy so that you can fully experience the love and freedom that is yours in Jesus Christ. I encourage you to fully engage in this process so that Christ can touch significant issues in your life — those of which you are aware and those of which you are unaware.

Hearing God / Receiving Healing

Jesus and Our Hurtful Past

All of us carry wounds from our past. Hurtful words, trauma, abuse, neglect, abandonment, demands for perfection, loss, poverty, rejection, addictions in the home, divorce, violence…all are the fabric of life in a fallen world.

As children, we take those experiences deep within us and often bear the wounds for years. As children, we come to conclusions about those events and why they happened to us. As children who cannot process the event as adults or through God's truth, we often take on beliefs about our worth, our competence, our goodness, and our destiny that are not true. Often, we adopt views of God as well that do not reflect the truth.

In addition, when we have been traumatized, we carry with us the memories of those moments that have painful emotions anchored to them. A familiar word, a look, a tone of voice, a remembered aroma, a certain sound — any of these can takes us back to the event, and in many ways we relive in the present the fear, rejection, sorrow, or pain of the past. These wounds are often doors through which the enemy gains access. Sometimes, he comes in at the moment of trauma through fear, shame or anguish. Sometimes, he comes in later through the unforgiveness and bitterness that we hold toward those who hurt us. When these wounds are healed, those doors are shut. Healing the wounds is the challenge.

We most often try to heal the wounds by denying the pain, locking away the memories, or giving ourselves pep talks about getting over it and getting on with life. At other times, we try to excuse or minimize what has happened to us because we still have to live with the people who hurt us. Ultimately, these are ineffective ways to heal these deep wounds. Even when we have forgiven those who wounded us, the lies about our own value, significance and competency remain, creating their own pain.

The most healing experience we can have is to talk to Jesus about those wounds. Paul prayed that God would give the believers in Ephesus *the Spirit of wisdom and revelation* (Eph. 1:7) that they might know him better. He also prayed that the *eyes of their hearts might be enlightened* (Eph. 1:18) so that they might know their hope, their riches in Christ, and the power that God was willing to exercise on their behalf. The deepest healing comes through revelation when Jesus speaks to you, sharing his love and his truth with your heart. Learning to meet Jesus in prayer and meditation and to hear from him is critical to our healing. Remember, Jesus came to heal the brokenhearted and he is willing to heal your heart.

A Meeting Place

In his book, *Can You Hear Me?* Brad Jersak speaks of meeting Jesus in prayer. He defines that meeting as a spiritual encounter where we meet Jesus to "behold or be held."[1] It may be a place to fix our eyes on Jesus or simply to receive his touch. Think of prayer as a place to meet God rather than a spiritual activity that you perform to please him or to deliver to him a "shopping list." Meeting God is the thing. Becoming aware of his presence and interacting with him in intimate fellowship is the goal.

In Revelation 1:10, John tells us that on the Lord's Day he was "in the Spirit." As he was in the Spirit he received the Revelation of Jesus. His experience of *being in the Spirit* was not just about being in God's Word or praying in tongues, although both of those things may have been involved. It was, more than likely, a state of mind or spirit in which he was meeting with Jesus to "behold or be held."

John was communing with the Lord — not just speaking but also receiving. John undoubtedly was in a state of mind or spirit in which he was ready to not only hear from the Lord but to see what Jesus might choose to show him including a revelation of himself. I'm not suggesting that Jesus will give us a new revelation to add to the cannon of scripture, but that Jesus is willing to reveal himself to each of us as he chooses — when we are open and expectant. I am not encouraging anyone to construct an image of Jesus as he or she sees fit or to simply plug in a cultural icon. Simply ask Jesus to reveal himself to you as he chooses and then wait patiently and expectantly for him to respond. "He who loves me will be loved by my Father, and I too will love him and show myself to him" (John 14:21).

As we pray and reflect on God's Word, we can then ask Jesus to meet us as a friend to share his heart with us. This is not a new age approach to spirituality but a centuries old path of encountering God. This is not emptying your mind and inviting in whatever spirit is in the neighborhood.

This is being directed by the Word and the Spirit of God and inviting one person to join you there — Jesus.

As mentioned earlier, Paul's constant prayer for the church in Ephesus was for the "the eyes of their hearts to be enlightened." How do we see with our hearts? How do we "fix our eyes on Jesus" (Heb. 12:12)? How do we "behold his glory" (2 Cor. 3:18)? How do we "see Jesus" (Heb. 2:9)? All of these passages, and more, speak about seeing the Lord or beholding him rather than just reading about him, thinking about him, or talking about him.

We, like John on the Lord's Day, are to behold him in our hearts, which is to say that we are to invite Jesus to reveal himself to us through our sanctified imagination. Think how often the Holy Spirit draws us into an image that we begin to project on the interior screen of our heart. The entire Book of Revelation is a vision that God wants us to vividly project and consider through our imagination. Ezekiel paints a picture of God coming in the clouds, riding his war chariot, carried along by cherubim with massive wheels intersecting massive wheels. Isaiah points us to a scene of the Lord high and lifted up, surrounded by Seraphim declaring his holiness. David takes us to green pastures and still waters. Jesus himself sketched scenes of farmers sowing seed, a shepherd feverishly leaving his flock to search after one, bridesmaids running to look for lamp oil, or Lazarus staring across a great gulf that separated him from a rich man suffering sweltering torment.

Are we not to enter into each of these scenes in our imagination which, when submitted to him, leads us to a revelation of truth from the Spirit? Do we believe that God gave man the faculty of imagination just so that he could invent, write fiction, or paint pictures on canvas for the marketplace? Isn't it more likely that he gave us an imagination so that his Spirit could paint the things of God — the things of heaven — on a canvas that we could behold... even the glory of God or the person of Jesus? When God communicates through dreams or visions, is not the imagination the screen on which these messages from God are projected?

Certainly, as we move into this realm, there is a chance of being deceived, of hearing and responding to a voice or an image that is not from God. But the possibility of deception lies in every approach to God. The enemy has deceived many who never sought to hear his voice or seek his face at all. No matter in which arena we seek to discover God, the Holy Spirit is the guardian of truth. Indeed, we are to test the spirits and the voice to see if it belongs to our true Shepherd. Jesus promised that his Spirit will lead us into all truth and remind us of all he has taught us. The Spirit will authenticate the Word of God, whether it comes in written form, thoughts, or visual representations on the canvas of our hearts.

If we are truly seeking Christ and his truth, and we are inviting Jesus and he alone to enter the door we have opened that we might share a spiritual meal with him, how can we trust the Holy Spirit to preside over that and sound the alarm if what we are hearing and seeing is not of God? Often, deep inner healing is dependent on hearing Jesus and, perhaps, even seeing Jesus as he speaks to us about the moments when our wounds were inflicted and the seeds of the enemy's lies were sown.

What does Jesus look like? No one knows for sure. It is amazing that four detailed biographies were written about Jesus and not one offered a physical description of him. After his resurrection, he appeared to many peoples and these witnesses saw him differently. Mary thought he was the gardener outside his tomb. Two disciples on the road to Emmaus did not recognize him at all. Even as the eleven ate fish with him on the shores of Galilee, he did not appear to them as the Jesus they would recognize by physical appearance.

He will show himself to you as he chooses, but in the context of past wounds, we simply want to ask Jesus to meet with us that we might be healed. In all of the New Testament, there is no record of Jesus refusing to heal anyone who asked. So, in faith, ask him now to lead you into his healing presence.

A Simplified Healing Process

Where there has been wounding and trauma, a significant place for healing is in that memory or in that past experience. Like cleaning out any wound that has not healed properly, you must revisit the sight, reopen the wound, and clean out the infection and any debris that may still be festering there. You must then apply antibiotics and a clean dressing for it to fully heal. That is true with emotional healing as well.

General Approach

We often want to make our relationship with Jesus more complicated than it is. We think, like Naaman the leper, that we must go through some arduous process to receive healing, when often it is as simple as dipping in the Jordan River. It is simple because God is good. He desires to heal his people. It is his name. In general, simply ask the Holy Spirit to guard your mind and your heart as he directs you to the most significant experiences related to your brokenness.

It may be an experience you clearly remember or one that you have neatly locked away. Prayerfully ask Jesus to go with you as you revisit that past experience in your imagination. Revisit the moment of wounding or a snapshot moment that represents the many times you were wounded. Picture in detail the people who were there, the colors, the smells, and the sounds that surround the moment of your rejection, betrayal, or shame. See yourself in that moment and ask Jesus to join you there. Ask him to speak to you about that moment. Ask him all the questions you have wanted to ask since that experience from long ago or not so long ago. That's it. When Jesus speaks, healing occurs — whether his words are spoken over a lame man or a broken heart.

As you approach Jesus for healing I would encourage you to begin with a time of personal worship to center your focus on him, his love for you, and his goodness. Remind yourself in faith that Jesus came to heal the brokenhearted. Find a place where you won't be disturbed. Ask Jesus to come and sit with you. When you sense that Jesus has prepared your heart…pray.

Important:

If you sense that you are going to revisit a memory that is filled with pain or fear, ask one or two trusted friends or mentors who are spiritually mature and sensitive to God's leading to sit with you and pray with you as you revisit your past.

Initial Prayer for Healing

Lord Jesus, you know the pain, hurt and confusion I often feel. You know the walls of self- protection I have built to cover my fear and my shame. You know how I struggle to give and receive love as you intended. I know that something in me is not in agreement with you. I know that strongholds exist in me that are beyond my ability to tear down.

Jesus, you are love and compassion, forgiveness and healing. Nothing is too hard for you. You are Jehovah Rophe — the God who heals. You are my Savior, my Redeemer, my Strong Tower, my Good Shepherd. You have all authority in heaven and on earth and a name that is above every name. Lord Jesus, I ask you to tear down every stronghold, to demolish every argument and every pretension that rises up in me and sets itself against your truth. Lord, break them down and in their places, by your Spirit, establish strongholds of your truth and love that the enemy can never penetrate.

Lord Jesus, I know that brokenness is not what you desire for me. You came to heal the brokenhearted, to replace sorrow with joy, despair with hope, captivity with freedom, darkness with light, and to restore the hearts and lives of your people. Jesus, I know that your truth will set me free. Speak your truth to me. Speak over my broken places and the lies the enemy has sown in those places. Jesus, I need your touch now to heal the wounds deep in my heart — even those I cannot see myself, but that you see. Lord, I pray for your Spirit of revelation and healing to be released in me and, by faith, I declare that by your wounds, I have been healed.

In the name of Jesus, I forgive those who wounded me and release them from the debt they owe. I entrust them to you, Lord Jesus, and ask that you bless them as you see fit. I now receive your truth, your joy, your peace, your love, your revelation and my healing, in Jesus' name. Jesus, I entrust myself to you and give you full permission to touch every place in me that needs cleansing, healing or forgiving. I hold nothing back and submit every part of my life to you.

I now lift up the lies I have believed: my anger, my fear, my shame, and my rejection, and give them to you. Holy Spirit, I plead the blood of Christ over my wounds for healing and release these lies and this pain to you, to be nailed to the cross. Jesus, wash me in your blood. Wash away my pain, my shame, my deceptions and the lies I have believed for so long. Lord Jesus, according to your promises, your love and your mercy — cleanse me from their effects. Fill me with your truth, your love, your peace, your approval, and your joy. I ask all these things in your name, Lord Jesus...Amen.

[Now it is time to revisit your past experiences.]

Holy Spirit, you are the guardian of truth. Protect me from any interference from the enemy as I seek the Lord's truth and healing. Jesus, I ask that you command the enemy to be silent and to stay away as we visit my past together.

Jesus, you are Lord of my past, present and future. Will you now take me to the birthplace of my brokenness? Will you bring to my mind my most needful memory for healing and freedom? Jesus, will you join me there now?

- Bring into focus the memory that the Spirit of God has raised up in you.
- Remember the details.
- Who is present? What are they wearing?
- Where are you? What are the colors in the scene? What are the smells or sounds around you?
- Picture yourself in that moment.
- What is happening to you or being said to you? What are you feeling? What are you thinking? What are you experiencing?

Ask Jesus...

- Jesus, where were you when this was happening to me?
- What were you feeling about what was happening to me?
- What do you want me to know about that experience?
- Jesus, how do you feel about me?
- What else do you want to say to me about that moment or about me?
- Lord Jesus, you are my healer and my Good Shepherd. Will you now take away my pain and my confusion, my fear, my anger, my shame and my self-loathing, and fill me with your love and your peace?

Write down what he says to you or shows you.

Ask Jesus if there is another memory that you need to visit at this time. If so, go through the same process for visiting past experiences until you hear or sense that you have done all he wants you to do today. There may be more for another day. If so, go through the same process with Jesus when you feel led to do so.

Write down whatever you hear or see from Jesus or whatever you experience with him.

Finally, thank Jesus for the truth he has spoken to you and for the love he has expressed to you. Ask his Spirit to write his truth on your heart so that you will never forget it.

End Notes
1. Brad Jersak, *Can You Hear Me?* (Grand Rapids: Monarch Books, 2008), p. 121.

OVERCOMING
DEMONIC OPPRESSION

D emons or unclean spirits come to do the work of Satan: to kill, steal and destroy (John 10:10). If they cannot prevent us from giving our hearts to Jesus, they will work to undermine our faith by stealing the word of God. They will work to create doubt, accuse God, and accuse us. They will harass, torment, condemn, disrupt relationships, attack our bodies, and tempt us to sin — all to draw us away from Christ or to cripple us and make us ineffective. Demonic spirits are not the cause of every hurt, emotional disturbance, disease or hardship in our life. We live in a fallen world with bodies subject to decay, illness, and damaged genes that have been impacted by the same processes. But demons do exist and experience tells me that they are the source of pain, bondage, compulsions and broken relationships in believers to a much greater degree than is usually acknowledged.

They come to us through our own un-repented sin, through wounds, through trauma, through curses and through bloodlines. They come and stay because something or someone has given them the legal right to afflict us. The process we are about to embark upon takes away their legal standing so that we, in the authority of Jesus, can command these spirits to leave.

Through the years, I have drawn on the teaching and books of numerous men who have helped the church understand and step into the arena of spiritual warfare where demonic spirits must be confronted. Don Basham, Derek Prince, Neil Anderson, Henry Malone, Ed Murphy, Francis MacNutt and others have effectively led thousands to freedom in Christ through their teaching, writing, and ministries of deliverance over the past two to three decades. Each has approached his own ministry in some unique way but there are common themes and approaches that seem to be present in everyone's ministry. Those common areas are, I believe, a firm place to stand as you begin to step into this arena.

The truth is that because of the victory already won by Christ, believers do not need to fear the demonic. Rather, the demonic should fear believers. We are not attempting to win the victory in our strength but are simply enforcing the victory that has already been won. Having said that, this is serious work where we should always stand on firm ground with the armor of God and the authority of Christ in place as we face the enemy.

In this section, we will be addressing fourteen spirits that are referred to in scripture. Spirits become evident through their fruit in our lives. In the same way that the Holy Spirit bears his fruit in our lives, such as love, joy, and peace unclean spirits bear their unholy fruit of fear, rejection, anger, manipulation, sexual immorality, addictions and so forth. Demonic influence is suggested when a believer seems to no longer have the ability to resist these sinful and destructive influences even though the believer often hates what he is doing, thinking or feeling. Often a believer who is experiencing demonic affliction has seemingly done all the right things to overcome a sin or an issue (prayer, more time in scripture, counseling, etc.) without making significant progress.

Deliverance is simply the process of identifying and uprooting a spirit by the power and authority of Jesus Christ. Once the spirit's legal ground has been taken away and the spirit is cast out or uprooted, the fruit will wither and die.

I believe that every sin named in scripture has a demonic spirit that is identified with it and that tempts man to "take and eat" of that sin. But, as a systematic approach to "cleaning house" the spirits identified specifically in scripture provide a thorough inventory of unclean spirits that most often need to be addressed. Because of that, this section will walk you through the systematic process of deliverance from each of these spirits, In doing so, you will learn a basic approach for deliverance that you may use in dealing with other unclean spirits as the Holy Spirit directs you.

Often there are spirits working in conjunction with one another. We know that Mary Magdalene was set free from seven spirits. The Gerasene man of Luke

8 was host to "Legion," who identified himself that way because there were many demons afflicting the man. Where more than one spirit is present, there is usually a commanding spirit that may be one of those named in scripture. These spirits seem to represent categories of harassment or oppression which suggests that they possess broad bands of authority over lesser spirits. They organize the strategies and give orders to other demonic spirits as they afflict an individual or family.

Just as the angelic hosts operate in military fashion with ranks and strategies, demonic spirits also function with strategy and organization. There are lines of authority and greater and lesser spirits within the kingdom of darkness. The demon who spoke through the Gerasene man who lived among the tombs identified himself as *Legion,* which was a Roman military designation. In the book of Daniel we are told that the angel who was sent to Daniel was resisted by the prince of Persia. Then Michael, one of the Lord's *chief princes,* came to fight against the demonic prince of Persia. This same Michael led the army of the Lord in war against the devil and his angels in Revelation 12. These chief princes, or "archangels," are commanders or generals in the army of heaven. The prince of Persia was a commander in the legions of hell. Within an individual who is afflicted by more than one spirit, there will typically be a commanding or organizing spirit.

Once this commanding spirit is cast out, the others (if they are present) can be dealt with more easily. For instance, there may be a commanding spirit of jealousy with lesser spirits of envy, insecurity, anger, etc. working to bear that fruit in our lives. At the core is *jealousy* but these other "symptoms" may be the work of other spirits. Often, lesser spirits simply leave with the commanding spirit as he is cast out.

As an initial step, you may find it helpful to always address these commanding spirits named in scripture. Then you will be able to deal with the lesser spirits if they are present or remain. You most often will know which spirits are present by the fruit they are manifesting as well as by the leading of God's Spirit. **I encourage you to have one or two spiritually mature men or women who will pray with you or have experience in deliverance as you walk through this process the first time.** Remember the proverb, "Though one may be overpowered, two can defend themselves. A cord of three strands is not quickly broken" (Ec. 4:12). Additional faith, wisdom and insight can be of great value as you face the enemy.

Spirits that have been present for years or generations can be resistant to eviction. It is not unusual for these spirits to argue against your demands, ridicule what you are doing, declare that Christ has no authority over them, and encourage you to abandon your "foolishness." You will experience these as thoughts and internal debates or even emotions. You may experience feelings of fear or sorrow that are not coming from you but from a spirit that is terrified of losing his place. Having spiritually mature individuals with you can help you stay focused, enable you to continue to command these spirits by faith, and strengthen you to persist in the name of Jesus.

Regardless, as a follower of Jesus Christ, you have the authority of Christ with which to command these spirits, once their legal ground has been removed. You are not commanding the enemy in your own strength or authority but as a representative of the King of Heaven. In his name, you can command the spirits to leave your spiritual "house" or the house of another.

There is no need to fear the enemy. "The one who is in you is greater than the one who is in the world." (1 John 4:4) The one you serve has "all authority in heaven and on earth." You stand in: "his incomparably great power for us who believe. That power is like the working of his mighty strength, which he exerted in Christ when he raised him from the dead and seated him at his right hand in the heavenly realms, far above all rule and authority, power and dominion, and every title that can be given, not only in the present age but also in the one to come. And God placed all things under his feet and appointed him to be head over everything for the church, which is his body, the fullness of him who fills everything in every way." (Eph. 1:19-23)

Notice that this immeasurable power is "for us" and "for the church." It has been given to Jesus so that he might wield it on your behalf. In addition, his Holy Spirit is within you and is jealous for you, even as God is. In Hebrews 1:14, Scripture declares that angels are ministering spirits sent forth to minister to those who will inherit salvation. That is you. As angels fought against the demonic for Daniel, they will do so for you. Ask Jesus to command his angels to be present with you and to enforce those things that you declare in Jesus' name.

As we minister deliverance on a regular basis, those with the gift of spiritual discernment are often aware of angels being present in the room with us. More than the presence of angels is the presence of Christ himself. Jesus is certainly with you for he in is in you and said that he will be with you even to the end of the age (Matt. 28:20). The Lord also promised that "where two or three are gathered together in my name, there am I in the midst of them" (Matt. 18:20) and the Father himself has promised that he will "never leave you nor forsake you" (Heb. 13:5).

As a final note, you may see that with some of the spirits named in scripture, we are told that God *sent* those spirits to certain men or to a nation. You may wonder why God is doing such a thing and whether we may be working against God if we cast out those spirits. God is not evil nor is he the source of evil. John tells us that "God is light and in him is no darkness at all" (1 John 1:5). However, God may eventually allow those who ignore his warnings and persist in sin and rebellion to experience the full consequences of their own choices. He may allow them to fully experience the law of sowing and reaping.

Satan is always poised to kill, steal or destroy. God's hand restrains the enemy. Satan complained that God had erected a hedge (a protective barrier) around Job that denied Satan access to him (see Job 1:10). The psalmist declares that the "angel of the Lord encamps around those who fear him" (Ps.34: 7) and we are promised that no weapon formed against us by the evil one will prosper (see Isa.54: 17). God typically restrains the enemy so that he cannot come against us with all of his fury.

When scripture says that God *sent* an unclean spirit it is a way of saying that God lifted his hand of protection and gave the enemy access to those who persistently refused to repent or hear God.

There are times when God lets a man (or nation) taste the real bitterness of the fruit he thought was sweet so that his heart might turn back to God. Sometimes, we turn over certain areas of our lives to Satan by loving a sin, excusing it, or denying responsibility for it. If we continually insist on aligning ourselves with Satan in that area of our life, God may have to honor our choices by removing any hedge he has placed around us so that we can taste the bitterness of sin and return to him.

However, God is love and quick to move again on our behalf when our hearts turn back to him. God's purpose in *sending* (releasing) an unclean spirit is to bring us to repentance. When his purpose for that spirit is accomplished he is quite willing for that spirit to be cast out by the authority of Jesus Christ. Little deliverance occurs when a heart still loves the sin an unclean spirit promotes in that heart. But great deliverance occurs when we have truly turned to God and hate the sin that hinders our relationship with him.

Taking an inventory of past events and patterns can point to demonic strongholds, curses, and soul ties that need to be broken by the power of Jesus Christ. As you work through the declarations in the rest of this book that pertain to spirits named in scripture, you will see that each one begins with a list of indicators that suggest the presence of that spirit or associated spirits. Highlight any of those indicators that suggest pockets of demonic activity in your life so that you may focus on those spirits especially as you advance through the process of deliverance.

Please remember that these declarations are not formulas or incantations. They are simply one expression for removing legal ground from the enemy, declaring the authority of Christ over these unclean spirits, and claiming the promises of God provided through the cross. In general you will (1) declare faith in and allegiance to Jesus, (2) renounce Satan and all of his the works in your life, (3) forgive those who have wronged you, (4) confess and repent of your own sins and the sins of your fathers, (5) nullify any curses, misdirected vows, or soul ties that have given the enemy access to you, (6) command the unclean spirit to leave immediately and never return, and (7) reclaim those things that have been taken from you by the enemy as you claim those things that are rightfully yours because of the exchange Jesus made with you on the cross.

You may also want to read further about demonic activity and deliverance before you proceed. If so, I recommend these books to you.

Deliverance from Evil Spirits by Francis MacNutt (Grand Rapids: Chosen Books, 1998)

They Shall Expel Demons by Derek Prince (Grand Rapids: Chosen Books, 1998)

The Bondage Breaker by Neil Anderson (Eugene, Oregon: Harvest House, 1990)

Shadow Boxing by Henry Malone (Lewisville, Tx., Vision Life Publications, 1999)

The Handbook for Spiritual Warfare by Dr. Ed Murphy (Nashville, Tn.: Thomas Nelson Publishers, 1992)

REMOVING LEGAL GROUND
FROM THE ENEMY

The following declarations and prayers will align you with Jesus in all these matters and take away any legal standing the enemy might appeal to in order to continue his harassment. All declarations and prayers should be spoken. These have the weight of legal testimony in the spiritual realm that should be declared openly if possible.

First, you should declare your faith and allegiance to Christ as you also renounce the works of Satan, which begins your alignment with Christ.

Prayer and Declaration of Faith

Father in heaven, I freely declare my faith in and my allegiance to Jesus Christ. According to your Word, I believe that Jesus Christ is your Son, that he lived a sinless life in the flesh and that he died in my place, taking my sin and my guilt upon himself. I believe that he was raised from the dead on the third day and ascended to heaven, where he was given all authority in heaven and on earth and a name that is above every name. I believe that at your word, he will return to claim his own while judging the wicked.

I believe that by his sinless life and by his resurrection, he defeated Satan and has broken his power and the power of sin in my life. I declare that by his blood, I am forgiven and by his sacrifice, I have been given his righteousness so that I am fully acceptable to you. I declare that I am saved by grace and by no righteousness of my own and that I am totally dependent upon Jesus in all that I do.

I now renounce sin and all the works of Satan. I acknowledge Jesus as my Lord and Savior and am committed to live for him each day of my life. I declare that your Holy Spirit lives in me and I freely submit myself to him to be transformed into the image of Jesus Christ. Thank you for making me your child by the blood of your Son and, in the name of Jesus, I receive total forgiveness for my sins and rejoice in your grace.

Your Word declares that you will never leave me nor forsake me. Your Word declares that Jesus will be with me even to the end of the age. Jesus, your Word declares that where two or more are gathered in your name you will be in their midst. Your Word declares that you came to heal the brokenhearted, and to proclaim freedom for the captives and release from darkness for the prisoners. Lord Jesus, in your name, I ask that you fulfill your purposes in me now for healing, for revelation, and for freedom.

Jesus, I ask that at this time you manifest your power, your authority and your healing in me. I plead your blood over my past, my present and my future, and ask that your Spirit will lead me and fill me. I thank you now for the healing and the freedom that you have promised and submit every part of my life and being to you. I entrust my soul, my spirit and my body to you and invite you to do whatever is needed to accomplish your purposes in me. May your will be done in me on earth as it is in heaven. It is in the name of Jesus I pray...Amen.

Secondly, declare your standing in heaven, which assures your right to operate in the authority of Jesus and the kingdom of heaven.

Declaration of Identity
In the Name of Jesus ....

I renounce the lies of Satan and his accusations that come against me. I renounce the lies that I am a slave to my brokenness, weakness, worthlessness, and displeasing to my Heavenly Father. In the name of Jesus and by his blood, I renounce shame, worthlessness, inadequacy, rejection, guilt, accusation and condemnation, because in Jesus Christ, I am totally loved, accepted, valued, and competent.

In the name of Jesus and according to the Word of God, I now declare that ...

I am a child of God — a beloved member of his household (John 1:12).

I am royalty in the household of God...chosen by Christ, adopted by the Father, anointed by his Spirit and sealed by the King (2 Cor. 1:22-23).

Because I am a child of God, washed in the blood of Jesus, I can come before the throne of grace at any time with great confidence and expect his help in time of need (Heb. 4:16).

Because God loves me, I have been bought at an incredible price and belong to him totally (1 Cor. 6:19-20).

I have been chosen to be a personal friend of Jesus Christ (John 15:5).

I am a branch of the true vine, Jesus Christ. His power, love, grace and authority flow into me, through me and into the world (John 15:1,5).

I am totally united to the love of God in Christ Jesus and nothing can separate me from that love — neither death nor life, angels nor demons, nor any powers (Rom. 8:35-39).

I have been declared innocent of all sin by the blood of Christ (Rom. 5:1).

I am free forever from all condemnation and any condemnation is a lie from the evil one (Rom. 8:1).

I am joined with Christ and his Spirit and I am made holy by that union (1 Cor. 6:17).

I am a saint, a holy one of God, set apart for his service (Eph. 1:1).

I lack nothing for godliness and love because I have been made complete in Jesus Christ (Col. 2:10).

I have not been given a spirit of fear but of power, love and self-control (2 Tim 1:7).

Because I am in Christ, I am a new creation, a servant of righteousness, and free from the power of sin (2 Cor. 5:17).

In everything, I am more than a conqueror though Jesus Christ (Rom. 8:37).

Because I am his, God is for me — the enemy cannot stand against me (Rom. 8:3l).

I am never alone because God has said, "No matter what, I will never leave you, I will never forsake you" (Heb. 13:5).

By faith in Christ, I have been set free from sin and am a willing slave to righteousness (Rom. 6:18).

As a follower of Jesus, I am a citizen of heaven. I am seated with Christ in spiritual realms, and by him, I have been given power and authority over the enemy. I am empowered to tread on scorpions and snakes because my King has all authority in heaven and on earth and is the Commander of the armies of Heaven (Luke 10:19; Eph. 2:6; Phil. 3:20; Matt. 28:18; Rev. 19:11-16).

In the name of Jesus, I renounce all lies to the contrary and in his name and by his blood, renounce and nullify all curses and judgments that have been spoken against me contrary to God's declared truth. Holy Spirit, will you now write these truths on my heart so that they cannot be stolen? In Jesus' name, I pray these things...Amen.

Thirdly, taking away legal ground from the enemy and moving in the authority of Christ means submitting every part of your life to Jesus. Unless you forgive others for their offenses against you, the Father will not forgive your offenses against him. By forgiving others, you take away the legal right of the enemy to harass you if you have been out of God's will in this critical spiritual matter.

Reflect on the names of people who have wronged you. List the names of the individuals you have not forgiven or for whom you have not declared your forgiveness. Ask the Lord to raise up in your mind any others for whom you need to declare forgiveness. Write them down and refer to them as you pray a prayer to forgive others.

Prayer to Forgive Others

Heavenly Father, your Word declares that if I forgive those who sin against me, you will also forgive me when I have sinned against you. I do so now. I do this in response to your mercy and grace toward me; for you forgave the unpayable debt of sin I owed you.

And so Heavenly Father, in the name of Jesus, I freely forgive (speak their names) _____ for any and all wrongs done to me.

In the name of Jesus, I release these individuals from their debt just as you released me. I require no payment for the wrongs done and release them to you for your righteous judgment. In response to your grace in my life, I choose to no longer act in any ways that are designed to make them pay for what they have done to me. I do this in recognition of the debt I could never repay, that you forgave through your Son.

Now, according to your Word, I release them to you. As I do so, in the name of Jesus, I also release anger, rage, bitterness, resentment, malice and all thoughts of vengeance to you and ask you to nail those thoughts to the cross. In the name of Jesus, I ask that you bless those who have wronged me and bring healing to my emotions so that in the days ahead, I may have the heart of Christ toward them.

Jesus, will you now bring to mind any other person(s) that I have not forgiven so that I may forgive them in your name and receive healing from you for the wrongs done to me?

I ask these things in the name of Jesus...Amen.

Having forgiven others, it is time to confess your sin and the sins of your fathers so that God, who is faithful and just, will forgive your sins and cleanse you of all unrighteousness (1 John 1:9). Check your inventory of unrepented sins and any sins of your fathers of which you are aware. Be ready to confess them in the following prayers.

Prayer for the Forgiveness of Personal Sins and Sins of the Fathers

Heavenly Father, in the name of Jesus, I confess my sin and my rebellion before you. At times I have willfully chosen to rebel against you and your Word. I have fallen short of your standards. At other times I have sinned against you, unaware. I declare that your standards are holy and just and renounce and repent of all my sin, known and unknown.

At times I have chosen to think and act in ways contrary to your will and your Word. I have no excuse and no one to blame. I have sinned against you and in the name of Jesus, I now renounce and repent of the sin(s) of _____

_____

_____

In the name of Jesus, I also confess the wickedness, the sins, and the rebellion of my fathers. I now renounce their sins, their wickedness, and their rebellion and submit those to the blood of Jesus that their affects might be nullified according to your Word. Specifically, I renounce _____

_____

Have mercy on me, O God, according to your unfailing love. There is nothing I can do to pay the debt of my sin and so by faith, I plead the blood of Jesus over my sin. Your Word declares that when I confess my sins with godly sorrow, you will be faithful and just to forgive me my sin and to cleanse me from all unrighteousness.

By the blood of Jesus, I ask you to blot out all my transgressions, wash away all my iniquity, and cleanse me from my sin. Your Word declares that in Christ, sin will not have dominion over me and I now come into agreement with your Word.

I turn away from my sins and the sins of my Fathers and receive the power of the cross through which I am crucified to the world, and the world is crucified to me. By your grace and by the blood of Christ I am now dead to sin — my own sin and the sins of my fathers._____

From this day forward, with your power, I will walk in freedom, no longer submitting to sin but to the righteousness of Christ. I now submit every area of my life to the Lordship of Jesus. Jesus, I ask that you totally break the power of this sin in my life that I might serve you wholeheartedly.

I now joyfully receive your promise of forgiveness by faith and give you thanks. Your Word declares that in Christ there is no condemnation and so I renounce the condemnation and the accusation that the enemy would speak against me and I declare that I am free in Christ from sin and the condemnation of sin.

In Jesus' name, I declare my complete forgiveness...Amen.

If you sense that there are any past hurtful or sinful relationships that still influence you or restrict you, pray for the breaking of soul ties in these past relationships. Pray over each relationship in which you participated willingly or unwillingly in sin, including traumatic experiences such as abuse, molestation or rape. Make a list of the people to whom you sense you may have ties in the spiritual realm from which you need to be released. Refer to those in the following prayer.

Prayer for Breaking Soul Ties

Heavenly Father, I come to you in the name of Jesus made righteous by his blood. I thank you that you are Lord over my past, present, and future. I thank you that you have given all authority in heaven and on earth to my Lord and High Priest, Jesus Christ. In the name of Jesus, I confess and renounce all past sins in which I have been willingly or unwillingly involved.

In particular I renounce the sins of _____
_____
_____

In the name and by the blood of your Son, Jesus Christ, I ask your forgiveness for the sins I willingly participated in and I ask cleansing for the sins that I participated in unwillingly. I also confess ungodly covenants and relationships that I established in my past, intentionally and unintentionally, that were contrary to your will. I renounce those covenants and renounce all my past sinful and destructive relationships that were not submitted to you.

Now, in the name of Jesus, by his blood, and by his authority I ask you to cancel all covenants from my past that were not godly covenants and I ask you to sever, by the sword of the Spirit, all ties that may have been established between me and

(name those who still influence your thoughts, feelings, decisions in negative ways)

_____

_____

    In Jesus' name, I now place these relationships under the Lordship of Jesus and under his blood and declare my complete freedom in him. Jesus, thank you for forgiving my past and for setting me free. May I walk only in your will in my relationships in all my days to come.

    It is in your name I pray…Amen.

    It is now time to break any curses that have been established by your sin, the sins of your Fathers, your declarations or the declarations of others.

Prayer for Breaking Curses and Vows…

Lord Jesus, I believe that you are the Son of God and the only way to God — that you died on the cross for my sins and rose again that I might be forgiven and receive eternal life. I now renounce all pride and self-righteousness. I have no claim on your mercy except your unfailing love for me that moved you to die on the cross in my place.

    Jesus I have confessed, renounced, and repented of all my sins and the sins of my fathers, known and unknown, and have knowingly withheld nothing. In your name I renounce these sins and every work of Satan. By a decision of my will, I have freely forgiven all who have ever harmed or wronged me. I surrender all anger, bitterness, resentment and revenge to the cross and, because of you, Jesus, I no longer require any payment for the wrongs done to me. I now release all judgment to you, the righteous judge.

    Lord, I thank you that on the cross you became a curse for me, that I might be redeemed from every curse and inherit God's blessings. I thank you that there is no condemnation for me because in Christ I have been set free from the law of sin and death. On the basis of your sacrifice for me, I now renounce every curse or judgment ever established against me based on my sin, the sins of my fathers, or words spoken by others or myself. Now by the blood, the name, and the promises of Jesus Christ I cancel every curse or judgment making them null and void. Also by the blood and the name of Jesus I cancel and nullify any demonic assignments associated with those curses.

In the name of Jesus, I also renounce any and all vows that I knowingly or unknowingly made in my past that were not aligned with God's will and purposes. By the blood of Christ, I cancel these vows; I declare them null and void, without influence in my life, and by the sword of the Spirit I am severed from their effects.

Jesus, thank you for becoming a curse, that I might be blessed. I ask you now, on the basis of your blood, to establish these things I have spoken in your name and loose me from any curse, vow or covenant that has given Satan access to me and my family. I ask you, by your authority and by the power of your blood, to establish my freedom from these things that have hindered my walk and your blessings in my life. I also ask that you seal off any entry points that may have given the enemy access in my past.

Jesus, thank you for setting me and my family free, that we might now receive the blessings you have purchased for us with your blood. I declare these things in your name...Amen.

DELIVERANCE

Deliverance occurs when an unclean spirit (demon) releases his hold on an individual or ceases his harassment and leaves the person. When you have come into alignment with Jesus by submitting every part of your life to the blood and the authority of Christ, then Satan's legal right to have a presence in your life is nullified. When this has been accomplished, believers (including you) may command these spirits to leave, by the authority of Jesus Christ.

As you command spirits to leave you should have faith that they are doing so because you are commanding in the authority of the King of Kings and Lord of Lords. They may exit without you experiencing any physical or sensory sensation. You will simply know they have gone when you realize that something is different in your life over the next few days or weeks. You may simply sense that something has left you or that you feel "lighter."

There also may be more concrete manifestations of a *spirit leaving* or a *spirit struggling to maintain his place in you*. These manifestations may be subtle or not so subtle. They may be seen by others or just experienced by the one being delivered. They may include…

- Physical sensations of pain or discomfort in the body that move around and then cease. These may include headaches, nausea, tightness of the chest, muscle pain, tingling in the arms or legs, etc.

186

- Yawning, coughing, gagging
- Inner peace, a quiet mind, and inner harmony for the person
- Immediate cessation of obsessive thoughts or intense emotions
- Unusual clarity of mind
- Joy
- A feeling of "lightness" and freedom
- Physical healing
- A sense that something has "left you"

Many times, unclean spirits will depart at your first command. At other times, they may resist. The gospels say in several places that Jesus and his followers "drove out" unclean spirits. If spirits resist your command, continue to declare Christ's authority over them until they comply and you (or the person to whom you are ministering) has a sense that the spirit has left or experiences a manifestation that confirms it.

Exercising authority does not require shouting, threatening, or extreme behaviors on the part of the individual commanding the spirits. Deliverance in the name of Jesus is not a power encounter but an authority encounter. Authority directs power. The authority given to believers directs the power of heaven which is unquestionable greater than that of hell. What we declare in the name of Jesus, when we are fulfilling his commands, will be established by the power of heaven (Job. 22:26-28). Those who have authority are confident in their authority and speak with authority — usually in firm, commanding tones but not with shouting and screaming. Jesus often spoke "sternly" to these spirits.

If a spirit speaks through the host, there is little benefit in having a conversation. Command the spirit to be quiet and comply with your commands that are being given in the name and authority of Jesus. Since Satan is a liar and the Father of Lies, those he commands are also liars. There is no point in talking to a spirit that by nature is a skilled liar and manipulator. Never get into a conversation or debate with Satan. Adam and Eve had such a conversation and look where we are today! Even Jesus, in his wilderness encounter with Satan, refused a conversation. He simply declared God's truth over Satan's manipulations.

When deliverance has been accomplished, end with a prayer thanking Jesus for the freedom he has provided for you. Ask him to fill you with his

Spirit and to seal off any access points in you or the person to whom you are ministering so that these spirits cannot return.

Remember the words of Jesus in the gospel of Luke. "When the unclean spirit has gone out of a person, it passes through waterless places seeking rest, and finding none it says, 'I will return to my house from which I came.' And when it comes, it finds the house swept and put in order. Then it goes and brings seven other spirits more evil than itself, and they enter and dwell there. And the last state of that person is worse than the first." (Luke 11:24-26)

Watch carefully what you do, those you choose to spend time with, what you read, and what you watch. Ask the Holy Spirit to fill every place left vacant by these spirits. Immerse yourself in the Word, prayer, praise and godly things. Be careful to give the enemy no entry points into your soul.

If old feelings or thoughts begin to "knock on your door," it may be old habits in the flesh but it may be another spirit attempting to move in. Treat the thought or feeling first as a spirit. Renounce the thought or feeling. Declare your allegiance to Jesus and then take authority over that spirit and command it to leave. Then, say "No!" to your flesh. Submit that vulnerable part of you to Jesus for his care, protection, and transformation.

Demons and Multiple Personality Disorder (MPD) or Dissociative Disorders

Sometimes, individuals who have been severely traumatized cope with the trauma by developing a number of "personalities" as part of their internal world. These alter "personalities" may or may not be aware of other personalities that exist in the mind of the traumatized individual. These "personalities" manifest at different times and may present themselves as individuals with names, histories, differing ages and genders.

These "personalities" are not demons but a psychological condition that has arisen to help the individual cope with the unbearable pain of their trauma. Although demons may also be present in these individuals, having gained access through the trauma, individuals with this disorder should not go through standard deliverance processes but need to work with Christian counselors who have training and experience in this area. If you suffer from MPD or any Dissociative Disorders, please tell someone who we can direct you to the proper resources.

Deliverance

Finally, you have aligned yourself with Christ in every area of your life, severed ungodly soul ties and nullified curses to which demonic spirits were assigned. It is time to exercise your delegated authority over any unclean spirits that have been a source of affliction, harassment, or oppression in your life. You may exercise your authority over every spirit listed below and over any other spirit of which the Lord makes you aware.

As you review the indicators, mark those that clearly have been part of your life if you have not already done so. Give special attention to those spirits that seem to strongly manifest in your life. Remember you are exercising authority in the name of Jesus, your Lord, your Savior, the King of Kings and Lord of Lords who commands the armies of heaven. He that is in you is greater than he that is in the world and his angels are present to enforce your declarations. You may make declarations over only the spirits you believe have oppressed you or you may do a thorough "house cleaning" by making declarations over every unclean spirit listed below. I recommend the house cleaning. Now, simply work through the prayers and declarations remaining in this book.

PRAYERS AND DECLARATIONS FOR DELIVERANCE

Jesus, your Word declares that you have all authority in heaven and earth and that you have a name that is above every name — in this age and the age to come. When you walked this earth you demonstrated your power over the enemy and cast out every kind of demon. You demonstrated your victory over Satan and hell by your resurrection because the grave could not hold you. You ascended from hell to heaven with those who had once been captive.

Jesus, according to your Word, I have repented of the sin in my life, I have forgiven all those who have ever wounded me, I have nullified every curse, every vow, and every covenant that was not aligned with the Father's will by the power of the cross and the blood you shed for me. By the power of your name and your blood, I have taken away any and all legal ground that the enemy may have had in my life. Thank you for breaking Satan's power in my life and for nullifying any legal claims he may have had to oppress my family or me.

In your name, I now renounce sin and anything satanic. No evil spirits have any right to me. By your blood, I cancel their legal right to have access to me and serve them notice that by the blood and the name of Jesus Christ, they are cast down. I declare that they are defeated in every part of my life. I declare that Satan is defeated by the blood and the resurrection of Jesus Christ and that Jesus has all authority in heaven and on earth. As a follower of Jesus Christ, a citizen of heaven, and a child of the King, Jesus has appointed me and anointed me with his power and authority over the enemy.

Jesus, I now ask you, as the Commander of the armies of heaven and as the Rider on a White Horse — King of Kings and Lord of Lords, to surround me with your angels and your presence and enforce your will as I command these unclean spirits to leave.

In the name of Jesus and by his authority, I now establish authority over any and every unclean spirit that has afflicted me or my family. By the blood of Jesus Christ, I have taken away all legal standing you have ever had to harass or afflict me. By the blood of Jesus I cancel every demonic commission that has been assigned to me or my family. I command you now to be silent and cease all activity. I forbid you from communicating with any other spirit or from crying out for help. In Jesus' name, you will be silent and inactive. You have no power here and no rights here. You will remain silent and inactive until you are called out and then you will leave immediately, bow at the feet of Jesus, and receive orders from him. As you leave, you will come out in an orderly manner without disrupting or disturbing and without afflicting or harassing any other person in this place. I command this in the name of Jesus.

Review the indicators of each demonic spirit's activity in your life. For those indicated, declare your Christ-given authority over them and command them to leave in the name of Jesus, the one who has all authority in heaven and in earth. You may want to do so for every spirit so that nothing is left undone since many of us are unaware of some demons that subtly influence our thoughts and emotions.

Spirit of Antichrist

"And every spirit that does not confess that Jesus Christ has come in the flesh is not of God. And this is the spirit of the Antichrist, which you have heard was coming and is now already in the world." (1 John 4:3)

You may experience this spirit as an unwelcome rejection and denial of truths about Jesus, which you experience as compelling thoughts that argue against the truth or that mock or ridicule truths about Christ. You may also experience this as consistent emotional "push back" against these truths. In addition, this spirit may produce feelings of anger or agitation when Jesus is honored in worship, word, or conversations. It may also manifest as religion or legalism that focuses on rules or an organization as a source of salvation rather than Jesus.

More indicators of this spirit are thoughts or emotions that...

- Deny essential truths about Christ: his deity, incarnation, resurrection, victory over Satan, etc.
- Persecute or slander the church or other believers.
- Oppose God's Word, bring an argumentative spirit to Bible studies, etc.
- Blaspheme the work of the Holy Spirit — attributing his work to Satan or denying its validity.
- Champion or give credibility to false religions and cults.
- Work to damage the Body of Christ and cause divisions.
- Exalts something or someone over Christ (self, intellect, organizations, philosophy or ideology).
- Deny the works and the power of God.

Declaration for Deliverance from Antichrist

Spirit of Anti-Christ, *I speak to you in the name and the authority of Jesus Christ who has all authority in heaven and on earth. I command you in the name of Jesus to release your hold on me now. By the power of his resurrection I break your chains and nullify any authority you have ever had in my life. In the name of Jesus and by his blood, I renounce you, bind you, and cast you out. You have no standing in my life and no legal claim against me. You are defeated and hurled down as Satan was hurled to earth from heaven. I now tear down every stronghold by the mighty name and the authority of Jesus Christ, by the power of his resurrection, and the power of the cross.*

By the authority of Jesus Christ, I command you, **spirit of Antichrist,** *to leave me now and to never return. Go immediately to the feet of Jesus and await his orders. I command you to go quietly and without incident — afflicting or harassing no one else as you go. By faith in Jesus Christ, I now take back everything the enemy has ever stolen from me and renounce, nullify, and uproot any and every lie sown in my heart by this unclean spirit.*

In Jesus' name, I now renounce all doubt, false doctrines, and the deceptions of Satan. Through the Holy Spirit, I now receive the mind of Christ, his truth, his Lordship, his discernment, and declare myself free in him to serve in faith, truth and righteousness. I surrender my heart and my intellect to you, Jesus, for your keeping and your perfection. In Jesus' name, I declare all these things and entrust them to him. Lord Jesus, I ask that you now enforce these things I have declared in your name and establish them by your power. Amen.

Spirit of Deaf and Dumbness

"When Jesus saw that a crowd was running to the scene, he rebuked the evil spirit. 'You deaf and dumb spirit,' he said, 'I command you, come out of him and never enter him again.' (Mark 9:25-27)

This spirit manifests in many different ways. It is primarily associated with an inability to hear or speak — either in the physical or spiritual realm. Those with this spirit may experience confusion when trying to read the Word or understand and process spiritual truths. It blocks understanding and revelation. It may also be connected with blindness and even seizures as it affects our mind's ability to process and blocks pathways to seeing, hearing or speaking in the physical and spiritual realm.

This spirit is often seen as a spirit of confusion or a "mind-binding" spirit. This spirit is sometimes connected to learning disabilities, attention deficit disorder, dyslexia, memory conditions, concentration, spiritual deafness, and physical deafness. Though you have ears to hear, you cannot hear. It may enter through rebellion, un-repented sin, unbelief or it may be passed down through generations as it often manifests in children.

More Indicators of this spirit are...
- Convulsions, seizures or epilepsy
- Deafness
- Muteness
- Dulling of the senses, reasoning, spiritual discernment
- Disease of the eyes and ears
- Inability to hear from God.
- Mental illness (schizophrenia, insanity)
- Suicidal attempts and tendencies

- Learning disabilities
- Inability to read Scripture or to understand it, even at basic levels

Declaration for Deliverance from Deaf and Dumbness

You **deaf and dumb spirit**, *I speak to you in the name and the authority of Jesus Christ who has all authority in heaven and on earth. I command you in the name of Jesus to release your hold on me now. By the power of his resurrection I break your chains and nullify any authority you have ever had in my life. In the name of Jesus and by his blood, I renounce you, bind you, and cast you out. You have no standing in my life and no legal claim against me. You are defeated and hurled down as Satan was hurled to earth from heaven. I now tear down every stronghold by the mighty name and the authority of Jesus Christ, by the power of his resurrection, and the power of the cross.*

*By the authority of Jesus Christ, I command you **deaf and dumb spirit,** to leave me now and to never return. Go immediately to the feet of Jesus and await his orders. I command you to go quietly and without incident — afflicting or harassing no one else as you go. By faith in Jesus Christ, I now take back everything that the enemy has ever stolen from me and renounce, nullify, and uproot any and every lie sown in my heart by this unclean spirit. By the blood of Jesus, I am now set free from any physical manifestations of this spirit, from confusion, and from all spiritual blindness and deafness.*

In the name of Jesus, based on his blood that was shed for me, through the Holy Spirit I now receive freedom, divine health, the mind of Christ, spiritual discernment and a conquering spirit, for I am more than a conqueror in Jesus Christ. In Jesus' name, I declare all these things and entrust them to him. Lord Jesus, I ask that you now enforce these things I have declared and establish them by your power. Amen.

Spirit of Stupor

"Just as it is written, 'God has given them a spirit of stupor, eyes that they should not see and ears that they should not hear, even to this day.'"
(Rom. 11:8)

This spirit manifests as dullness and lethargy: spiritually or physically. It appears as dulled senses and dulled sensitivity, unresponsiveness, apathy, sleepiness, laziness, or bewilderment. This spirit may gain entrance through constant discouragement as a child, through curses or vows spoken over the child related to failure and lack of success, or through words spoken that instilled an identity of being lazy, no good, a loser, etc. It may also gain entrance through rebellion and stubbornness toward authority… especially God's.

More Indicators of this spirit are…

- Lack of ambition
- Inability to succeed
- Constant fatigue — emotionally or physically
- Passivity
- Procrastination
- Self-pity
- Isolation and withdrawal
- Forgetfulness

Declaration for Deliverance from Stupor

Spirit of stupor, I speak to you in the name and the authority of Jesus Christ who has all authority in heaven and on earth. I command you in the name of Jesus to release your hold on me now. By the power of his resurrection I break your chains and nullify any authority you have ever had in my life. In the name of Jesus and by his blood, I renounce you, bind you, and cast you out. You have no standing in my life and no legal claim against me. You are defeated and hurled down as Satan was hurled to earth from heaven. I now tear down every stronghold by the mighty name and the authority of Jesus Christ, by the power of his resurrection, and the power of the cross.

*By the authority of Jesus Christ, I command you **spirit of stupor** to leave me now and to never return. Go immediately to the feet of Jesus and await his orders. I command you to go quietly and without incident — afflicting or harassing no one else as you go. By faith in Jesus Christ, I now take back everything the enemy has ever stolen from me and renounce, nullify, and uproot any and every lie sown* *in my heart by this unclean spirit. By the blood of Jesus, I am now set free from any work or manifestation of this spirit.*

In the name of Jesus, based on his blood that was shed for me, through the Holy Spirit I now receive energy, strength, healing, passion, godly ambition, zeal, diligence, success, focus and confidence. In Jesus' name, I declare all these things and entrust them to him. Lord Jesus, I ask that you now enforce these things I have declared and establish them by your power. Amen.

Spirit of Error

> *"We are from God, and whoever knows God listens to us; but whoever is not from God does not listen to us. This is how we recognize the Spirit of truth and the spirit of falsehood (error)."* (1 John 4:6, parentheses mine)

The spirit of error leads us into beliefs about Christ that deny scriptural truth. This spirit appeals to our intellect or our cultural biases and gives greater weight to our worldly way of thinking than to Scripture. Satan usually candy-coats his lies in partial truths, but at the core are concepts or beliefs that lead us away from Christ. The spirit of error always wars against our full reception of the truth, leaving us in unbelief and doubt.

This spirit will deny the deity of Christ (i.e. *The DaVinci Code*), the virgin birth, the resurrection, the humanity of Christ, and the truth of his teachings, or it will deny that we have accurate representations of his teachings, judgment to come, etc. The *spirit of error* will introduce "tolerance" and "compromise" into our faith, presenting Christ as one way to heaven but not the only way to heaven. This spirit may provide "spiritual experiences" designed to deceive us into believing that we are on the path of truth because we have had a spiritual experience. This deception can manifest as spiritual manifestations, "hearing from a spirit," angel worship, etc.

More Indicators of the presence of a Spirit of Error are...
- Anti-Semitism
- Moral or spiritual compromise
- Confusion
- Cult Involvement (Free Masonry, Eastern Star, Mormonism, etc.)
- Deception
- Doubt

- False doctrines
- False prophecy and teaching
- Inappropriate immaturity, behavior or thinking, especially in spiritual matters
- Intellectualism, spiritual pride and arrogance
- Persistent unbelief
- Self-righteousness
- Rejection of the Church and disdain for other believers

Declaration for Deliverance from Error

Spirit of error, I speak to you in the name and the authority of Jesus Christ who has all authority in heaven and on earth. I command you in the name of Jesus to release your hold on me now. By the power of his resurrection I break your chains and nullify any authority you have ever had in my life. In the name of Jesus and by his blood, I renounce you, bind you, and cast you out. You have no standing in my life and no legal claim against me. You are defeated and hurled down as Satan was hurled to earth from heaven. I now tear down every stronghold by the mighty name and the authority of Jesus Christ, by the power of his resurrection, and the power of the cross.

*By the authority of Jesus Christ, I command you, **spirit of error,** to leave me now and to never return. Go immediately to the feet of Jesus and await his orders. I command you to go quietly and without incident — afflicting or harassing no one else as you go. By faith in Jesus Christ, I now take back everything the enemy has ever stolen from me and renounce, nullify, and uproot any and every lie sown in my heart by this unclean spirit. . By the blood of Jesus, I am now set free from any work or manifestations of this spirit.*

In the name of Jesus, based on his blood that was shed for me, through the Holy Spirit I now receive truth, understanding, wisdom, revelation, discernment, a sound mind, and humility. In Jesus' name I declare all these things and entrust them to him. Lord Jesus, I ask that you now enforce these things I have declared and establish them by your power. Amen.

Spirit of Lying

"Therefore, the Lord has put a lying spirit in the mouth of these prophets of yours, and the Lord has declared disaster for you." (2 Chr. 18:22)

A spirit of lying primarily prompts individuals to lie without compunction or conscience…even to the extent of believing that the lie they have told is actually true. The spirit provides justification for the lie or deceives the liar to the extent that he or she is no longer clear about the separation between reality and imagination. A lying spirit can also operate on a person to open that person up to lies, especially to believe what they want to believe, contrary to God's Word. The serpent in the Garden was functioning as a lying spirit and prompted Adam and Eve to doubt God and make disastrous decisions.

This spirit often enters in where individuals have chosen lying and manipulation as a way to get what they want or as a form of self-protection against abuse or rejection. When there is no confession and repentance, this spirit may establish a stronghold so that lying becomes an essential strategy in the person's life and so that the person feels totally justified in bending the truth for his or her purposes or protection. There is often victimization in their past and a sense of entitlement in their present that makes the individual feel justified in using people as repayment for the wrongs done to them.

More indicators of this spirit are…

- Accusations
- Condemnation toward others
- Controlling behaviors
- Deception
- Emotionalism
- Exaggeration
- Excessive talking
- Flattery
- Hypocrisy
- Lying
- Manipulation
- Perfectionism to project an image
- Religious pretense
- Strong Delusions
- Victim's mentality

Declaration for Deliverance from Lying

Spirit of Lying, I speak to you in the name and the authority of Jesus Christ who has all authority in heaven and on earth. I command you in the name of Jesus to release your hold on me now. By the power of his resurrection I break your chains and nullify any authority you have ever had in my life. In the name of Jesus and by his blood, I renounce you, bind you, and cast you out. You have no standing in my life and no legal claim against me. You are defeated and hurled down as Satan was hurled to earth from heaven. I now tear down every stronghold by the mighty name and the authority of Jesus Christ, by the power of his resurrection, and the power of the cross.

*By the authority of Jesus Christ, I command you, **spirit of lying,** to leave me now and to never return. Go immediately to the feet of Jesus and await his orders. I command you to go quietly and without incident — afflicting or harassing no one else as you go. By faith in Jesus Christ, I now take back everything the enemy has ever stolen from me and renounce, nullify, and uproot any and every lie sown in my heart by this unclean spirit. By the blood of Jesus, I am now set free from any work or manifestations of this spirit.*

In the name of Jesus, based on his blood that was shed for me, through the Holy Spirit I now receive truth, integrity, faith, single-mindedness, discernment, self-worth and a truthful tongue. In Jesus' name, I declare all these things and entrust them to him. Lord Jesus, I ask that you now enforce these things I have declared and establish them by your power. Amen.

Spirit of Fear

"For God did not give us a spirit of fear, but a spirit of power, of love and of self-discipline. " (2 Tim. 1:7)

This spirit often comes in through trauma, abandonment, violence, extreme poverty, or abuse. It may be passed on intergenerationally, by overprotective, fearful parents, or may come in through an environment of perfectionism where love and security are removed if a child's performance is never "good enough." Fear of rejection or abandonment is prevalent. It may be experienced as general anxiety, acute insecurities, panic attacks, fear of rejection, fear of conflict, fear of poverty, people pleasing, phobias, obsessive thoughts about death or injury, etc.

More indicators of the presence of this spirit are...

- Fear of abandonment
- Accusation: persistent thoughts of accusation toward self or others
- Anxiety
- Condemnation, especially thoughts of self-condemnation
- Critical spirit
- Faithlessness
- Fear of death
- Fear of failure
- Fear of poverty
- Fear of victimization
- Fright
- Inability to trust
- Inadequacy / Inferiority
- Legalism
- Migraines
- Nightmares / Night Terrors
- Orphan mind-set that always feels uncared for, alone, or helpless.
- Panic attacks / Paranoia / People-Pleasing / Perfectionism / Phobias
- Rejection, especially constant feelings of rejection
- Shyness
- Timidity
- Torments
- Worry

Declaration for Deliverance from Fear

Spirit of fear, *I speak to you in the name and the authority of Jesus Christ who has all authority in heaven and on earth. I command you in the name of Jesus to release your hold on me now. By the power of his resurrection I break your chains and nullify any authority you have ever had in my life. In the name of Jesus and by his blood, I renounce you, bind you, and cast you out. You have no standing in my life and no legal claim against me. You are defeated and hurled down as Satan was hurled to earth from heaven. I now tear down every stronghold by the mighty name and the authority of Jesus Christ, by the power of his resurrection, and the power of the cross.*

*By the authority of Jesus Christ, I command you, **spirit of fear,** to leave me now and to never return. Go immediately to the feet of Jesus and await his orders. I command you to go quietly and without incident — afflicting or harassing no one else as you go. By faith in Jesus Christ, I now take back everything the enemy has ever stolen from me and renounce, nullify, and uproot any and every lie sown in my heart by this unclean spirit. By the blood of Jesus, I am now set free from any work or manifestations of this spirit.*

In the name of Jesus, based on his blood that was shed for me, through the Holy Spirit, I now receive power, love, a sound mind, trust, faith, courage and the peace of Jesus Christ. In Jesus' name, I declare all these things and entrust them to him. Lord Jesus, I ask that you now enforce these things I have declared and establish them by your power. Amen.

Spirit of Jealousy

"... and if the spirit of jealousy comes over him and he is jealous of his wife who has defiled herself, or if the spirit of jealousy comes over him and he is jealous of his wife, though she has not defiled herself." (Num. 5:14, ESV)

This spirit often enters in through loss and rejection, abuse and feelings of unworthiness and insecurity. It manifests often as inappropriate anger or even rage when we feel rejected, disrespected, invalidated, minimized, accused, feel the threat of losing a relationship or feel the threat of rejection, etc. This spirit can be so intense as to prompt us to murder, as it did when Cain killed his brother.

More indicators of this spirit are...
- Anger that is frequent and unmanageable
- Abuse
- Blaming
- Comparisons
- Controlling behaviors (threats/manipulations)
- Covetousness
- Cruelty
- Distrust
- Divorce
- Emotional detachment

- Envy
- Feeling that God loves you less than others
- Hardness of heart
- Hate
- Insecurity
- Jealousy
- Rage (even to the point of Murders as when Cain killed Abel)
- Revenge
- Shame
- Self-absorption
- Suspicion

Declaration for Deliverance from Jealousy

Spirit of jealousy, *I speak to you in the name and the authority of Jesus Christ who has all authority in heaven and on earth. I command you in the name of Jesus to release your hold on me now. By the power of his resurrection I break your chains and nullify any authority you have ever had in my life. In the name of Jesus and by his blood, I renounce you, bind you, and cast you out. You have no standing in my life and no legal claim against me. You are defeated and hurled down as Satan was hurled to earth from heaven. I now tear down every stronghold by the mighty name and the authority of Jesus Christ, by the power of his resurrection, and the power of the cross.*

By the authority of Jesus Christ, I command you, **spirit of jealousy,** *to leave me now and to never return. Go immediately to the feet of Jesus and await his orders. I command you to go quietly and without incident — afflicting or harassing no one else as you go. By faith in Jesus Christ, I now take back everything the enemy has ever stolen from me and renounce, nullify, and uproot any and every lie sown in my heart by this unclean spirit. By the blood of Jesus, I am now set free from any work or manifestations of this spirit.*

In the name of Jesus, based on his blood that was shed for me, through the Holy Spirit, I now receive trust, security, contentment, gentleness, patience, peace, self-worth and love. In Jesus' name, I declare all these things and entrust them to him. Lord Jesus, I ask that you now enforce these things I have declared and establish them by your power. Amen.

Spirit of Haughtiness

"Pride goes before destruction and a haughty spirit before a fall." (Prov.16:18-19)

This spirit manifests as a belief in one's general superiority to others. It manifests in a belief that one's views are always superior and that one's needs are always more valid than others. It manifests in spiritual pride, boasting, and self-righteousness. It shows itself in a critical and judgmental spirit toward others. It dominates and controls, not out of insecurity, but out of a belief in superiority and entitlement. It is often arrogant and demands its way because it is always more worthy than others.

More indicators of this spirit are...
- Arrogance
- Bigotry
- Blaming others
- Bragging
- Critical spirit
- Contentiousness: always arguing or debating in order to be right or superior.
- Controlling / Domineering
- Egotism
- Gossip
- Judgmental spirit
- Inappropriate competitiveness (must win at any cost)
- Mockery
- Prejudice
- Pride
- Rudeness
- Sarcasm
- Scorn
- Self-righteousness
- Superiority
- Vanity

Declaration for Deliverance from Haughtiness

Spirit of haughtiness, *I speak to you in the name and the authority of Jesus Christ who has all authority in heaven and on earth. I command you in the name of Jesus to release your hold on me now. By the power of his resurrection I break your chains and nullify any authority you have ever had in my life. In the name of Jesus and by his blood, I renounce you, bind you, and cast you out. You have no standing in my life and no legal claim against me. You are defeated and hurled down as Satan was hurled to earth from heaven. I now tear down every stronghold by the mighty name and the authority of Jesus Christ, by the power of his resurrection, and the power of the cross.*

By the authority of Jesus Christ, I command you, **spirit of haughtiness,** *to leave me now and to never return. Go immediately to the feet of Jesus and await his orders. I command you to go quietly and without incident — afflicting or harassing no one else as you go. By faith in Jesus Christ, I now take back everything the enemy has ever stolen from me and renounce, nullify, and uproot any and every lie sown in my heart by this unclean spirit. By the blood of Jesus, I am now set free from any work or manifestations of this spirit.*

In the name of Jesus, based on his blood that was shed for me, through the Holy Spirit, I now receive humility, honesty, grace, transparency, respect, a submissive heart, regard for others, and security in Christ. In Jesus' name I declare all these things and entrust them to him. Lord Jesus, I ask that you now enforce these things I have declared and establish them by your power. Amen.

Spirit of Heaviness (Despair)

> *"To console those who mourn in Zion. To give them beauty for ashes, the oil of joy for mourning, the garment of praise for the spirit of heaviness."* (Isa. 61:3)

This spirit usually comes in through loss, poverty, and rejection, which produces a belief that life will never fulfill its promises or that an individual is unworthy of success, blessing, or love. It manifests as hopelessness about life, a sense of being "a loser," despair about situations, and a belief that things will never get better. It also appears as resignation, abandonment of dreams, constant discouragement, and a sense of inevitable victimization. It may also manifest as depression, suicidal thoughts, self-destructive behaviors, or inconsolable grief and sorrow.

Other indicators of this spirit are...

- Accusation, especially self-accusing thoughts
- Brokenheartedness
- Condemnation, especially feelings or thoughts of condemnation, unworthiness, or shame.
- Constant sorrow, unrelenting grief
- Depression / Despair / Constant Discouragement
- Hopelessness
- Inconsolable grief or mourning
- Loneliness
- Rejection
- Self-Pity
- Shame
- Unjustified guilt
- Unworthiness / Self-Loathing
- Wounded Spirit

These dark feelings may also prompt us to medicate the pain with food, sex, drugs, etc. working closely with bondage.

Declaration for Deliverance from Heaviness

Spirit of heaviness, I speak to you in the name and the authority of Jesus Christ who has all authority in heaven and on earth. I command you in the name of Jesus to release your hold on me now. By the power of his resurrection I break your chains and nullify any authority you have ever had in my life. In the name of Jesus and by his blood, I renounce you, bind you, and cast you out. You have no standing in my life and no legal claim against me. You are defeated and hurled down as Satan was hurled to earth from heaven. I now tear down every stronghold by the mighty name and the authority of Jesus Christ, by the power of his resurrection, and the power of the cross.

*By the authority of Jesus Christ, I command you, **spirit of heaviness,** to leave me now and to never return. Go immediately to the feet of Jesus and await his* *orders. I command you to go quietly and without incident — afflicting or harassing no one else as you go. By faith in Jesus Christ, I now take back everything the enemy has ever stolen from me and renounce, nullify, and uproot any and every lie sown in my heart by this unclean spirit. By the blood of Jesus, I am now set free from any work or manifestations of this spirit.*

In the name of Jesus, based on his blood that was shed for me, through the Holy Spirit, I now receive joy, gladness, peace, a heart of praise and thanksgiving, confidence, the hope of Jesus Christ, the comfort of the Spirit, acceptance, and significance found in the righteousness of Jesus. In Jesus' name, I declare all these things and entrust them to him. Lord Jesus, I ask that you now enforce these things I have declared and establish them by your power. Amen.

Spirit of Divination / Occult Spirit / Witchcraft

> *"...we were met by a slave girl who had a spirit of divination...Finally, Paul became so troubled that he turned around and said to the spirit, 'In the name of Jesus I command you to come out of her!' At that moment, the spirit left her."* (Acts 16:16, 18)

These spirits come to us by way of our own or our ancestor's occult involvement. This could include horoscopes, fortune-telling, Ouija boards, new age activities, séances, mediums, white magic, satanic cults, Wicca, witchcraft, tarot cards, etc. Occult spirits manifest in a number of ways that usually counterfeit the leading of God — directive thoughts, visions, dreams, seeing into spiritual realms, manifestations of demons, demonic activity in the environment, threatening thoughts, destructive thoughts, or suicidal thoughts.

It is important to evaluate the voices and experiences you are having to see if they reflect the nature and character of Christ, if what you are seeing and hearing is consistent with the Word of God, if what you are seeing and hearing exalts Christ and draws you closer to him, and if spiritual leaders sense that your experiences are from God. The objective of occult spirits is to draw you away from Christ and to motivate you to place your trust in things other than in Christ. They may entice you at first and feign friendship, but will move to oppression, fear, and threats to control you as they gain strength in your life. They will slander Christ and his church and create confusion about truth. Some occult experiences are covered with a mantle of Christianity and spirituality but create dependence on a man or a formula rather than Christ.

More Indicators *of the Spirit of Divination are desires to be involved in or actual experiences with:*

- Astrology
- Channeling
- Charms
- Crystals/ Crystal balls
- Demonic manifestations
- Diviners (fortune-tellers)
- Eastern religions
- Fascination with death
- Free Masonry or involvement in other cults
- Games (Satanic/Occult: Dungeons & Dragons, etc.)
- Horoscopes
- Incantations
- Magic (black or white)
- Mediums
- Mysticism
- Ouija Boards
- Palm readers
- Rebellion
- Satanic Worship
- Séances
- Sorcery
- Suicidal thoughts / Romanticized views of death
- Tarot cards
- Transcendental Meditation
- Witchcraft
- Etc.

Declaration for Deliverance from Divination

Spirit of divination, I speak to you in the name and the authority of Jesus Christ who has all authority in heaven and on earth. I command you in the name of Jesus to release your hold on me now. By the power of his resurrection I break your chains and nullify any authority you have ever had in my life. In the name of Jesus and by his blood, I renounce you, bind you, and cast you out. You have no standing in my life and no legal claim against me. You are defeated and hurled down as Satan was hurled to earth from heaven. I now tear down every stronghold by the mighty name and the authority of Jesus Christ, by the power of his resurrection, and the power of the cross.

*By the authority of Jesus Christ, I command you, **spirit of divination**, to leave me now and to never return. Go immediately to the feet of Jesus and await his orders. I command you to go quietly and without incident — afflicting or harassing no one else as you go. By faith in Jesus Christ, I now take back everything the enemy has ever stolen from me and renounce, nullify, and uproot any and every lie sown in my heart by this unclean spirit. By the blood of Jesus, I am now set free from any work or manifestations of this spirit.*

In the name of Jesus, based on his blood that was shed for me, through the Holy Spirit, I now receive faith, trust, a pure heart, spiritual discernment, a heart of worship, a heart of submission, and self-denial. In Jesus' name, I declare all these things and entrust them to him. Lord Jesus, I ask that you now enforce these things I have declared and establish them by your power. Amen.

Spirit of Bondage

"For you did not receive the spirit of bondage again to fear, but you received the spirit of adoption, whereby we cry, 'Abba Father.'" (Rom. 8:15)

This spirit is experienced as bondage, addictions, obsessive thoughts or compulsions. When a believer hates a behavior, has repented often, has asked God to take it away, and the behavior or thought pattern persists or even grows stronger, this spirit is indicated. This spirit may manifest in all kinds of ways but often is accompanied by shame, condemnation, a need to blame others for behavior we can't control, anger, etc. It most often comes in through wounds to our self-image and self-worth, and prompts us to medicate our feelings of unworthiness, inadequacy and rejection with destructive behaviors and substances.

More indicators of this spirit are...
* Addictions
  ◊ Substance abuse

◊ Alcohol

◊ Sexual (including all forms of pornography and masturbation)

◊ Nicotine

◊ Television

◊ Computer / Computer Games / Social Networks

◊ Food

◊ Exercise

◊ Gambling

◊ Shopping

- Eating disorders
- Obsessive activities
- Obsessive thoughts
- Relational addiction to another person
- Self-absorption (narcissism)
- Obsession with material possessions

Declaration for Deliverance from Bondage

Spirit of bondage, *I speak to you in the name and the authority of Jesus Christ who has all authority in heaven and on earth. I command you in the name of Jesus to release your hold on me now. By the power of his resurrection I break your chains and nullify any authority you have ever had in my life. In the name of Jesus and by his blood, I renounce you, bind you, and cast you out. You have no standing in my life and no legal claim against me. You are defeated and hurled down as Satan was hurled to earth from heaven. I now tear down every stronghold by the mighty name and the authority of Jesus Christ, by the power of his resurrection, and the power of the cross.*

*By the authority of Jesus Christ, I command you, **spirit of bondage,** to leave me now and to never return. Go immediately to the feet of Jesus and await his orders. I command you to go quietly and without incident — afflicting or harassing no one else as you go. By faith in Jesus Christ, I now take back everything the enemy has ever stolen from me and renounce, nullify, and uproot any and every lie sown in my heart by this unclean spirit. By the blood of Jesus, I am now set free from any work or manifestations of this spirit.*

In Jesus' name, I now renounce any and every form of bondage in my life. By the blood of Jesus, I break every addiction, nullify every compulsion, and submit every obsession to the Lordship of Jesus.

In the name of Jesus, based on his blood that was shed for me, through the Holy Spirit I now receive divine healing for any and every physical component of addiction, freedom, patience, peace, self-control, godly contentment, and an overcoming spirit, for I am more than a conqueror in Jesus Christ. In Jesus' name I declare all these things and entrust them to him. Lord Jesus, I ask that you now enforce these things I have declared and establish them by your power. Amen.

Spirit of Prostitution
(Sexual Immorality, Spiritual Adultery, Idolatry)

"My people inquire of a piece of wood, and their walking staff gives them oracles. For a spirit of prostitution has led them astray, and they have left their God to play the whore." (Hos. 4:12)

This Spirit will often manifest in sexual addictions and may join with a spirit of perverseness to take those addictions into even deeper levels of sin, brokenness, and shame. This spirit also leads people into idolatry and the worship of things that are not God. This spirit often gains access through sexual abuse, molestation, and pornography. Rejection, abuse or neglect may also create a lack of significance and self-worth in a person that pushes him to seek approval, notoriety, security, and the praise of men in various ways (idolatry), rather than turning to God to meet their needs or heal their wounds.

More indicators of this spirit are involvement in or strong, persistent temptations to be involved in....
- All forms of Sexual Immorality:
- Adultery
- Bestiality
- Excessive lust
- Exhibitionism
- Fornication
- Homosexuality
- Incest
- Habitual masturbation
- Molestation
- Pornography
- Promiscuity

- Prostitution
- Rape
- Seduction
- Sexual fantasies, particularly when obsessive or compulsive
- Idolatry
- Love of money
- Love of worldly things
- Love of social status
- Lust for fame
- Lust for power
- Trusting in people or things other than God for significance, identity, security, purpose, etc.

Declaration for Deliverance from Prostitution (Idolatry)

Spirit of prostitution, *I speak to you in the name and the authority of Jesus Christ who has all authority in heaven and on earth. I command you in the name of Jesus to release your hold on me now. By the power of his resurrection I break your chains and nullify any authority you have ever had in my life. In the name of Jesus and by his blood, I renounce you, bind you, and cast you out. You have no standing in my life and no legal claim against me. You are defeated and hurled down as Satan was hurled to earth from heaven. I now tear down every stronghold by the mighty name and the authority of Jesus Christ, by the power of his resurrection, and the power of the cross.*

By the authority of Jesus Christ, I command you, **spirit of prostitution,** *to leave me now and to never return. Go immediately to the feet of Jesus and await his orders. I command you to go quietly and without incident — afflicting or harassing no one else as you go. By faith in Jesus Christ, I now take back everything the enemy has ever stolen from me and renounce, nullify, and uproot any and every lie sown in my heart by this unclean spirit. By the blood of Jesus, I am now set free from any work or manifestations of this spirit.*

In the name of Jesus, based on his blood that was shed for me, through the Holy Spirit I now receive sexual purity, holiness, single-minded devotion, faithfulness, self-control, the mind of Christ, and goodness. In Jesus' name, I declare all these things and entrust them to him. Lord Jesus, I ask that you now enforce these things I have declared and establish them by your power. Amen.

Spirit of Perverseness

> *"The Lord has mingled a perverse spirit in her midst; and they have caused Egypt to err in all her work, as a drunken man staggers in his vomit."* (Isa. 19:14)

Biblically, this spirit causes people to act in ways that are opposed to God, and to twist and distort what is good. In a sense, this is the spirit that declares good to be evil, and evil to be good. It is an action or thought contrary to God's direction, but in a twisted, evil, or unnatural way. It may manifest as rebellion or stubbornness against God's clear directives or twist the nature of things and call it natural. It is often manifested in distorted views of God that would slander his character, sadistic manipulation of people, and in unnatural sexual relations.

More indicators of this spirit are...
- Argumentativeness
- Arrogance
- Distorted and manipulative views on religious issues
- False teaching
- Rebellion or stubbornness
- Gender confusion
- Sadistic behaviors and manipulations
- Sexual perversions
  - ◊ Homosexuality
  - ◊ Bestiality
  - ◊ Incest
  - ◊ Molestation
  - ◊ Sexual Abuse
  - ◊ Orgies
  - ◊ Sadomasochism
  - ◊ Pornography

Declaration for Deliverance from Perverseness

Spirit of perverseness, *I speak to you in the name and the authority of Jesus Christ who has all authority in heaven and on earth. I command you in the name* *of Jesus to release your hold on me now. By the power of his resurrection I break your chains and nullify any authority you have ever had in my life. In the name of Jesus and by his blood, I renounce you, bind you, and cast you out. You have no standing in my life and no legal claim against me. You are defeated and hurled down as Satan was hurled to earth from heaven. I now tear down every stronghold by the mighty name and the authority of Jesus Christ, by the power of his resurrection, and the power of the cross.*

By the authority of Jesus Christ, I command you, **spirit of perverseness,** *to leave me now and to never return. Go immediately to the feet of Jesus and await his orders. I command you to go quietly and without incident — afflicting or harassing no one else as you go. By faith in Jesus Christ, I now take back everything the enemy has ever stolen from me and renounce, nullify, and uproot any and every lie sown in my heart by this unclean spirit. By the blood of Jesus, I am now set free from any work or manifestations of this spirit.*

In the name of Jesus, based on his blood that was shed for me, through the Holy Spirit I now receive understanding, a sound mind, truth, humility, sexual holiness, a godly sexual identity, contentment, the mind of Christ, purity and goodness. In Jesus' name, I declare all these things and entrust them to him. Lord Jesus, I ask that you now enforce these things I have declared and establish them by your power. Amen.

Spirit of Death

> *"'Where, O death, is your victory? Where, O death, is your sting?' The sting of death is sin, and the power of sin is the law. But thanks be to God! he gives us the victory through our Lord Jesus Christ."* (1 Cor. 15:55-56)

Death is not clearly named as a demonic spirit, but it is directly addressed and nearly every individual who ministers deliverance treats it as a strong spirit that frequently needs to be dealt with.. The spirit of death manifests often as an obsession with an individual's own death or the death of someone he loves or that he has lost to death. It manifests as a fear of death and foreboding.

It may also show itself through a fascination with death or the demonic and even a longing for or romanticism about death. It may also express itself in suicidal thoughts. This spirit may also work to bring about death in a person's life, apart from God's appointed time. It may gain access to a person through traumatic events associated with death, abortion, occult involvement, generational suicide, and through curses spoken by an individual or parent concerning death or expressing a desire to die.

Other indicators of this spirit are...

- Attempted suicide or history of suicide in the family
- Frequent life-threatening accidents
- Eating disorders
- Cutting
- Other self-destructive behaviors

Declaration for Deliverance from a Spirit of Death

Spirit of death, *I speak to you in the name and the authority of Jesus Christ who has all authority in heaven and on earth. I command you in the name of Jesus to release your hold on me now. By the power of his resurrection I break your chains and nullify any authority you have ever had in my life. In the name of Jesus and by his blood, I renounce you, bind you, and cast you out. You have no standing in my life and no legal claim against me. You are defeated and hurled down as Satan was hurled to earth from heaven. I now tear down every stronghold by the mighty name and the authority of Jesus Christ, by the power of his resurrection, and the power of the cross.*

By the authority of Jesus Christ, I command you, **spirit of death,** *to leave me now and to never return. Go immediately to the feet of Jesus and await his orders. I command you to go quietly and without incident — afflicting or harassing no one else as you go. By faith in Jesus Christ, I now take back everything the enemy has ever stolen from me and renounce, nullify, and uproot any and every lie sown in my heart by this unclean spirit. By the blood of Jesus, I am now set free from any work or manifestations of this spirit.*

In the name of Jesus, based on his blood that was shed for me, through the Holy Spirit I now receive purpose, a love for life, wholeness, fruitfulness, destiny, joy, the peace of Jesus Christ, and abundant grace. In Jesus' name, I declare all these things and entrust them to him. Lord Jesus, I ask that you now enforce these things I have declared and establish them by your power. Amen.

Spirit of Infirmity

And behold, there was a woman who had a spirit of infirmity eighteen years, and was bent over and could in no way raise herself up. (Luke 13:11, NKJV)

This spirit primarily attacks the body and manifests as a disease or a physical condition. This is a strategy to limit and torment believers. Although all disease or physical conditions are ultimately caused by sin in the world, not all disease is demonic. Much is simply the result of living in an environment cursed because of sin and living in bodies that are also subject to sickness and decay.

However, scripture is clear that disease is the work of devil and that some diseases and conditions are demonic. A demonic presence gives "life" to the disease. It mimics natural diseases and conditions but is supernatural. When the demon is expelled, the disease or condition loses its source of being and, therefore, ceases to function in the body. This spirit may also come with a curse attached to un-repented sin, rebellion, or idolatry and is commissioned to see that the curse is fulfilled in the person's body.

More indicators of a spirit of infirmity...

- Any sickness or condition that does not respond to prayer, treatment, and healthy regimens.
- Persistent symptoms that cannot be diagnosed or that are often misdiagnosed.
- Recurring illnesses or conditions, including general fatigue, weakness, sickliness, as well as specific diseases and disorders — especially from generation to generation.

Sickness and infirmity are often the result of unresolved spiritual or emotional issues that compromise our immune system through stress caused by fear, worry, anger, unforgiveness, intense feelings of shame, or rejection, etc. These areas of our lives, that are out of agreement with God's truth, give the enemy access to us and our physical bodies. A constant discipline of asking God to reveal areas of our lives that are not in agreement with him, and then submitting those areas of thought and emotion to Christ, will often free us from infirmity and any spirit of infirmity that afflicts us.

Declaration for Deliverance from Infirmity

Spirit of infirmity, I speak to you in the name and the authority of Jesus Christ who has all authority in heaven and on earth. I command you in the name of Jesus to release your hold on me now. By the power of his resurrection I break your chains and nullify any authority you have ever had in my life. In the name of Jesus and by his blood, I renounce you, bind you, and cast you out. You have no standing in my life and no legal claim against me. You are defeated and hurled down as Satan was hurled to earth from heaven. I now tear down every stronghold by the mighty name and the authority of Jesus Christ, by the power of his resurrection, and the power of the cross.

By the authority of Jesus Christ, I command you, spirit of infirmity, to leave me now and to never return. Go immediately to the feet of Jesus and await his orders. I command you to go quietly and without incident — afflicting or harassing no one else as you go. By faith in Jesus Christ, I now take back everything the enemy has ever stolen from me and renounce, nullify, and uproot any and every lie sown in my heart by this unclean spirit. By the blood of Jesus, I am now set free from any work or manifestations of this spirit.

In the name of Jesus, based on his blood that was shed for me, through the Holy Spirit I now receive divine health in my body for "by his stripes I am healed." In his Name and according to his Word, I loose myself from infirmity and bind myself to the healing power of Jesus Christ. I receive Shalom, the peace and prosperity of Christ, in my body, my emotions and my mind. I receive strength, the abundant life of Jesus, and the fruit of the Spirit into my life. I come into agreement with his Word that declares, "he forgives all my sins and heals all my diseases." In Jesus' name, I declare all these things and entrust them to him. Lord Jesus, I ask that you now enforce these things I have declared and establish them your power...amen.

Final Declaration

Satan, you and all your demons are defeated and your power is broken this very day in my life. The old is past and the new has come. Jesus, thank you for dying that I might live. Thank you for becoming a curse that I might be blessed. Thank you for defeating the enemy that I might be set free. Strengthen me now to walk in this freedom and be pleasing to you in every way.

Jesus, I ask that you now fill me with your Spirit. Fill every place left vacant by the enemy and Jesus, by your Spirit, cover with your blood and seal every place that gave the enemy entrance into my life.

Holy Spirit, I ask that you now touch every wound in me and apply the healing blood of Christ to each one. I offer up my pain, my fear, and my emotions to the Lordship and the healing power of Jesus now. By his wounds, I am healed.

Thank you, Jesus, for all that you have done and will do in me because of your great love and faithfulness. I praise you and give you honor in all things. In your name I pray...amen.

FINAL WORD OF
ENCOURAGEMENT

The enemy will immediately come and attempt to steal your faith about the work of Christ in your life. He will whisper that nothing happened and that all of your efforts were foolishness and emotionalism. When the enemy comes, rebuke him in the name of Jesus, command him to leave your presence, and seal your deliverance and healing immediately with thanksgiving and testimony, declaring to someone else what Jesus did for you today.

Satan will also arrange for you to encounter people from your past or present whom he would use to draw you back into sin and brokenness. Do not think that you can handle their influence today. Avoid that person or find a reason to leave that encounter immediately.

You will also notice that you will be tempted by thoughts that want to take you back to the destructive behaviors and sin that bound you before today. First, treat that thought as a spirit —rebuke it in Jesus' name, and command it to leave and not return. Also know that the flesh wants to default back to its old ways. Just say "no" and declare what God would have you do or think instead of agreeing with your flesh.

Fill your life and the spiritual places left vacant through deliverance with the things of God. Increase your prayer, time in the Word, praise and Christian fellowship in the days ahead. If you feel that something is stirring or incomplete in your deliverance, go through the declarations and prayers again or contact some spiritual leaders to help you assess what is going on and to pray with you.   Grace and peace to you from the Lord Jesus Christ!

CPSIA information can be obtained
at www.ICGtesting.com
Printed in the USA
BVHW030842030419
544470BV00008B/1263/P

9 781614 486046